THERE'S A CRACK IN YOUR NEST EGG:

AN OWNER'S MANUAL FOR A SUCCESSFUL RETIREMENT

ANTHONY NEWMAN, PRESIDENT
LIFEGUARD FINANCIAL

This document discusses general concepts for retirement planning, and is not intended to provide tax or legal advice. Individuals are urged to consult with their tax and legal professionals regarding these issues. This handbook should ensure that clients understand a) that annuities and some of their features have costs associated with them b) that income received from annuities is taxable and c) that annuities used to fund IRAs do not afford an additional measure of tax deferral for the IRA owner.

Printed in the United States of America

First Printing, 2015

Gradient Positioning Systems, LLC
4105 Lexington Avenue North, Suite 110
Arden Hills, MN 55126
(877) 901-0894

Gradient Positioning Systems, LLC and Anthony Newman are not affiliated with or endorsed by the Social Security Administration or any government agency.

TESTIMONIALS

"Thanks for getting us on the right track to be financially secure."
                                    - Lydia and Tom Z. *Aurora, OH*

"Lifeguard has been a lifesaver for our retirement investments. We have the utmost confidence in Anthony Newman."
                                    - Ray and Rose I. *Largo, FL*

"I have been with Lifeguard Financial for over 16 years. Anthony Newman expertise strategies have helped to increase my retirement portfolio tremendously and I am happy that I have never lost any money!"
                                    - Nancy D. *Willoughby, OH*

"Doing business with Lifeguard Financial has always been a positive experience. Tony always gives his clients his personal attention. He has helped me by providing solutions to all of my concerns and has made the right decisions. It is apparent that he genuinely cares about his clients. He has been an outstanding advisor and has stayed on top of things. He gives me realistic expectations and always delivers on what he promises."

*- **Sandy T.** Phoenix, AZ*

"Joe and I have been clients of Lifeguard Financial for over 20 years. We have followed his advice and are quite pleased with our returns."

*- **Joe and Mary Ann V.** Painesville, OH*

"We feel that honesty and integrity are very important when dealing with money. Certainly Anthony Newman and his staff fully live up to this qualification."

*- **Frank and Phyllis A.N.** Royalton, OH*

"My 401(k) was invested in the stock market after I retired. I was on that roller coaster ride and lost a lot of money. I changed my investments to Lifeguard Financial and quickly recovered my losses. I have the highest confidence in Anthony Newman and Lifeguard Financial."

*- **Dave P.** Parma Heights, OH*

"How do I like you? Your accounts make me sleep better. Your interest and genuine concern to grow and protect my money helps me sleep better. And the money you have made me makes me live better. You have never disappointed me."

*- **Betty V.** Englewood, FL*

"I have been with Lifeguard Financial for many years. I was hesitant to change advisors, but it was the best decision I ever made. Tony is extremely knowledgeable, ethical and honest. I trust him completely. His staff is courteous, available, professional and helpful. They are never too busy for me."

- Peggy H. *Mentor, OH*

"Timely and professional service, excellent follow through, top notch supporting staff, immediate response to questions, responsive and compassionate to clients' needs and concerns."

- Frank S. *Naples, FL*

"Never did we realize what a good decision we made by going with Anthony Newman until the economy and stock market took a downturn. Our accounts showed an increase when most of our friends lost money. We feel safe and have confidence in Anthony Newman."

- Mark and Joyce L. *Broadview Heights, OH*

"I was with another stockbroker and was hesitant to make a change. But I went with Anthony Newman and Lifeguard Financial just before the dot coms crashed. His wise decisions and attention to my money have proven to be quite successful."

- George S. *Richfield, OH*

ACKNOWLEDGEMENTS

First and foremost, I would like to thank my wife, Kim, for standing beside me throughout my career. Her support, encouragement and advice inspired me to continually succeed. I would also like to thank my wonderful children, Brian and Britt, for their understanding, genuine interest in my career and patience. I hope this book makes them as proud of me as I am of each of them. I want to thank my staff, Stephen Christopher, Debbie Hurley and Shawn Harris. Their loyalty, dedication and ability to manage work overloads provided the necessary support to make both Lifeguard Financial and myself a success.

Equally important is the daily information and direction provided to me by the Gradient Financial Group; Chuck and Tami Lucius, Tony and Beth Compton, Chad Roesler, Jaime Malm, Sheri Mushel, Nick Stovall, Gretchen Beatty, Nikki and Jeff Foley, Brian Lucius, Tony Wald, Tony Shore, Alyse Snyder, Shawn

Travers, Nick Maryns, and Jake Kulju. They have been a contributory factor that has allowed me to achieve my goals year after year and to prosper.

And last but not least, a heartfelt thank you to my 1,600 clients in greater Cleveland, Florida and several other states for the confidence and trust that they have placed in Lifeguard Financial and myself, for the opportunity to grow and protect their money, and the chance to keep my promise regarding their expectations and our services.

TABLE OF CONTENTS

INTRODUCTION

Whether you are planning to retire or are already retired, you need to have a sound financial plan and periodically give it a tune-up. The world and stock market have changed drastically. Economist Harry Dent recently said, "investors who continue to speculate and don't control the risk in their portfolios may suffer losses and never recover." There are cracks in your nest egg that need to be fixed. Every financial plan has flaws. It's time that you take control!

Stock market losses, excessive spending, forced IRA distributions, taxation and paying too much in fees will eventually separate you from your money. Outliving your money is the number one concern of pre-retirees and retirees today. Getting a second opinion could stop you from making the same mistakes that were made in 2000 and 2008. By taking a comprehensive approach to planning your retirement, including a thorough analysis of your assets, you will know when you will run out of money, assuming you continue on your current plan.

The next step is to research basic principles that will allow your money to last as long as you and your spouse live, no matter what age. In addition, if there is a large loss of income upon the death of your spouse, the longevity income plan will more than replace your financial loss. The benefit of such a plan is that you don't have to rely on stock market returns or worry about losses. Your principal will never diminish and you won't have to wait years for interest rates to rise. Speculation comes at a price. You can't take two steps forward and one back and expect to prosper.

Don't underestimate what taking too much risk can do to your retirement plan. Strategies that protect and sustain your nest egg will help you to better prepare for and position yourself during retirement. With some careful planning, you may be able to replace your income deficit, recover market losses, structure a guaranteed lifetime pension and retire more comfortably, perhaps even earlier, than originally planned.

> *Troy's father worked for the same company for nearly his entire career. He had a pension, some savings, and of course his Social Security benefits. Troy's parents paid off their house, avoided credit card debt, and enjoyed a simple but comfortable retirement.*

Things are different today.

Troy has a 401(k) and an IRA, but he doesn't know what to expect from year to year. Will the market go up or down? Very few of the people he knows have a pension, and managing his personal finances seems much trickier than in his parents' day. When Troy talks to his friends and family about retirement, it seems they all share the same sentiment: things are much different today.

Money represents more than the paper it's printed on. It is the embodiment of your time, your talents, and your commitments. It buys the food you eat, the house you sleep in, the car you drive, and the clothes you wear. It also helps provide you with the lifestyle you want to live once you retire.

You have spent a lifetime earning it, spending it, and hopefully, accumulating it. When the time comes for retirement, you want your money to provide you with a comfortable lifestyle and stable income after your working days are done. You might also have other desires, such as traveling, purchasing property, or moving to be closer to your family, or further away. You may also want your assets to provide for your loved ones after you are gone.

The truth is that it takes more than money to fulfill those needs and desires. Your income, your plans for retirement, your future healthcare expenses, and the continued accumulation of your assets after you stop working and drawing a paycheck all rely on one thing: *You.*

The way you approach your retirement impacts your income, the taxes your assets are subject to, your financial stability in the future, and your legacy. It is a common saying among financial professionals that *one hour of organizing your assets can be worth more than an entire lifetime of working and saving* when it comes to retirement.

How is that possible? The fact of the matter is that after working and saving for a lifetime, entering retirement changes all of the rules you have known and followed for your entire career. Instead of an earning and saving paradigm, you are moving into an income and asset leveraging paradigm where you need to use the money you have earned and saved to generate income and preserve your assets. Making sure your assets last for your lifetime will depend on how you decide to invest them and in what order you will spend them.

With forces like inflation, market volatility, and fluctuating interest rates working against you, knowing what to do with your assets has never been more important. The difference between making a good decision and a bad decision has never had such a dramatic impact on how people retire.

The question isn't CAN you or SHOULD you put your money to work for you and your family. It's HOW you do it.

Along the way, you will meet people just like yourself. Hard-working, responsible people who are facing some of the same financial challenges you might be facing. This book isn't meant to provide easy, stock answers, but instead will equip you to ask the right questions and avoid some common mistakes.

RETIREMENT PLANNING DO's AND DON'Ts

The decisions you make **before** and **during** retirement will have either positive or negative consequences that will affect you, your family, your potential heirs, and your peace of mind for many years. Knowing what to do and what not to do can help guide your decisions about retirement.

The good news is that you can plan for your retirement. Focus on things that are within your control, such as risk, excessive fees and spending, and unnecessary taxes.

A sustainable stream of income for life is the goal when planning for retirement. Unfortunately, some people are left to face the prospect of returning to work after incurring profound losses to their retirement fund, which could have been prevented by minimizing the exposure to risk. Consider this: if yo u have $800,000 invested in a market that drops 20 percent, and you need $30,000 to meet your annual income needs, your balance will be $610,000. It is very difficult to recover. Don't chance it.

DON'Ts	**DO's**
Pick a retirement date by selecting a time because you become eligible for Social Security benefits, you reach a certain age or your house will be paid off.	Find out how much you need in savings and other structured assets in order to retire comfortably; determine the most efficient way to get to that number by calculating what rate of return you'll need to earn on your nest egg; find out how much you can withdraw monthly and still preserve your portfolio.
Leave retirement funds in an account with your former employer after you retire.	Take your money with you when you retire so that you have full control of your hard-earned nest egg. Develop a relationship with a local, reputable advisor who can help you determine the best course of action to take to protect and grow your portfolio.
Continue to expose your portfolio to the same amount of risk as you did when you were working. It can be harder to cushion the blow of losses without a paycheck or a company matching your 401(k) contributions. Suffering large losses in combination with necessary withdrawals for income could do irreparable harm to your nest egg.	Create a portfolio with a better mix of investments and minimal risk exposure. This type of portfolio will help you achieve reasonable goals for accumulation.
Take too much income or take it from the wrong accounts.	Create an income stream strategy about a year before you retire. A retirement planning specialist can help you determine what amount is needed, what accounts it will come from and whether you have enough money to provide yourself with that income into your 90s.
Retire with a lot of debt. You'll find yourself struggling to make ends meet instead of enjoying your time in retirement.	Retire debt-free so that your income can be used for your lifetime. Develop and implement a payment plan to pay off your mortgage, credit cards and other debts.
Think you're alone when it comes to the daunting task of planning for retirement or that professional advice is out of reach or unaffordable.	Seek guidance from a retirement planning specialist who can help guide you through financial, estate and tax planning. Focus on creating customized strategies to grow and protect your nest egg, decrease your taxes, and increase the wealth left for distribution.

STEPS TO MAKING YOUR RETIREMENT LAST

The prospect of outliving the assets in a retirement portfolio is a concern for many retirees and pre-retirees. You may be facing a fixed retirement date that has been chosen for you rather than a date you can control.

Today, retirees are living longer and are finding it challenging to grow their portfolios in today's challenging markets. Volatile investments, low fixed rates, and uncertainties about taxes have a huge impact on the investment decisions of today's seniors. Some investors think that making monthly withdrawals from their nest egg is the best and only way to provide income during retirement *but this strategy comes with serious and sometimes unforeseen financial consequences.* To avoid this, you must design a reliable way to receive income.

As you approach your prospective retirement date, it's certainly best to develop an efficient plan long before the date arrives. It's not too late for those who have already begun retirement to take advantage of some of these strategies, however.

Here's how to start:

- *Have funds available in a safe and liquid vehicle. Having too much on hand means your money is not working hard enough for you. To help create a viable income stream, excess funds beyond what you may need for everyday expenses and emergencies should be placed in tax-efficient investments such as tax-free bonds or the right annuities.*
- *Be cautious when looking to generate income from long-term bond funds. Advisors warn about this because when interest rates rise, prices fall and the principal amount suffers a loss.*
- *Know your expenses. The easiest way to track expenses is to simply write down what you spend monthly on things like health care, insurances, mortgage or rent transportation, taxes, utilities, food, etc. Try to include absolutely everything*

and then factor in a little more to this amount for the unexpected. The next step is to calculate your total monthly income including anything you receive from Social Security, pensions, dividends, IRA required minimum distributions, etc.

Once you subtract the total amount of projected expenses from the total amount of income, check to see if a deficit would be created in the event that a spouse should pass away and the income they are receiving is lost. If so, it is imperative that you prepare by establishing a longevity income plan now for the surviving spouse.

RESETTING YOUR FINANCIAL GOALS

Taking a new approach to your retirement will likely require a new set of goals. You will need to know exactly how much money you need to maintain your lifestyle in retirement, how to put your plan into action, and who to work with to accomplish your goals.

The following outline will help you start the process of rethinking your future financial goals:

- **Assess Your Current Financial Situation and Objectives**
    -How aggressive or conservative do you now want to be?
    -How much time do you have until you need money for income or a planned purchase?
    -Consider your age and projected longevity.
    -Do you need tax favored investments?
    -Understand or research how different investment vehicles work, their risk level, and cost.

- **Develop a Strategy in Order to Reach Your Goals**
    -Diversify, don't duplicate.
    -Monitor your progress regularly, at least monthly. Keep a log.
    -Create or adjust a savings or investment plan (i.e. save more, spend less).

-Plan for the unexpected (reduction in Social Security benefit, loss of spousal income, loss of employment, critical illness, etc.).

-Revise your budget every December for the approaching year.

-Clear up debt. Pay off your highest interest rates first, pay your mortgage bi-monthly, use charge cards only if you can pay the balance in full.

-Maximize work retirement plans and save more on your own.

-Set realistic expectations in these current financial and economic times. Cut losses sooner and make a new plan.

- **Select or Change Advisors**

  -You don't have to plan for retirement alone. Seek out a reputable advisor who listens to you, who can create a simple plan, and who is 100 percent transparent with fees. Before you commit, ask to see their plan in writing.

  -Get a second opinion if you are unhappy with service or results. With change comes improvement.

BUILDING YOUR RETIREMENT

From a purely financial perspective, the primary challenge of planning for a long, secure retirement is preparing for the day your paycheck stops and you need to turn a lifetime of savings into an income you cannot outlive. While this is a challenge you have never faced before, there are many ways to make your retirement dreams into realities.

Retirement is more than kicking back and cashing in on your Social Security. Not only are there many different options for each individual that affect when and how to file for Social Security benefits, there are many more for how to structure other assets like individual retirement accounts (IRAs), 401(k)s, life insurance policies, and investment portfolios. Each person's retirement is unique. Discovering the most efficient and effective way to leverage your assets for a comfortable retirement requires some elbow grease, the right tools and the help of a professional. Think of it like this: You took time to choose your career, your educational path, your employment experience, and the time and talent required to develop your professional skill-set. You chose a profession or a line of work that matched your skills and talents with your income needs and lifestyle choices. You did this to suit your needs and preferences, to give you the salary you desired, and to do the work you were interested in and good at performing.

Creating a retirement plan requires the same crafting and care that you put into your career. Your assets, your income needs, and your lifestyle are different from your neighbor's. You need a retirement plan that reflects your needs.

Even though you know that retirement is coming and you may have concerns as to whether you will have enough money to live comfortably once it arrives, not everyone takes the time or makes the effort to get the most from their retirement. Like a lot of complex decisions that lie ahead of you, it is easy to keep putting it off while other things in life capture your attention. Retired life is or soon will be your life, and just a little bit of planning with a trusted financial professional can help you keep living the life you want once you retire.

HOW DO I START PLANNING AND PREPARING FOR RETIREMENT?

Your lifestyle, your desires, and your idea of how you want to live are all factors that will shape the way you structure your investments to deliver the retirement you want. So, how can you get a handle on your retirement and create a plan that draws on the strength of *diversity* and *planning*?

To build anything, you need to have three things: a plan, a process, and the help of a professional. If you built or bought a house, you probably had a vision of what you wanted, a time frame within which you needed it completed, and the skilled labor of a professional contractor to guide you through the design and build process, or a real estate agent to show you properties that met your specifications. More than likely, you knew what you wanted your house to be like and how you wanted to use the space. You needed the architectural and design skills of a contractor to help give shape to the layout of your home, or the listening skills of a realtor to help select houses that fit your vision. Designing, building, and choosing your retirement follows the same recipe. You may know what you want, and a professional knows how to help you get you there.

Most people spend more time planning their vacations than they spend planning for their retirement. While this seems almost unbelievable, the fact is most people have a vague understanding of what they need to do to plan ahead for retirement. Not knowing what to do or how to plan for it makes it easy to avoid or put it off for later. But sometimes later never comes, and many people find themselves applying for their Social Security benefit before they reach the age of maximum payout of their Social Security benefit, exposing their 401(k)s or IRAs to high levels of market risk, and living on a fixed income that doesn't afford them the lifestyle they desire or are accustomed to enjoying.

The basic roadmap to retirement looks like this:

Organize your assets. Organize your finances, assets, obligations, and liabilities, and make them simple to understand. This can start with a simple list of the financial product(s) you own and a list of your debts and other obligations. A financial professional will help you sort out the value of each asset, the beneficiaries that are listed for each one, and how much risk each asset is exposed to. That last component, the risk assessment, will play a very important role in how you structure your retirement plan.

Your financial professional may also be able to help structure your plan to help you retire your debts and other obligations.

Create an income plan. The first thing you'll need on day one of your retirement is a reliable income. When your paycheck stops coming in, you still need to pay the bills. Understanding how much income you need each month and where it will come from will form the foundation for the rest of your retirement.

Accumulation. After your income needs are met, you have the opportunity to take your additional assets and leverage them for profit to provide you with income in the future, to prepare for anticipated health care costs, and to contribute to your legacy.

Taxes. Understanding how taxes affect your retirement income and accounts will help you make decisions that can save you money and protect your legacy.

Creating a Legacy. Creating a lasting legacy requires making smart financial decisions. Taking inventory of your assets with a professional will help ensure that your listed beneficiaries are up to date, that you have a strategy for covering health care costs, funeral expenses, and strategies for avoiding costly probate proceedings and tax penalties.

Finding a Financial Professional. Working with a financial services professional to craft your retirement is one of the smartest decisions you can make. The peace of mind that comes with working with someone you can trust who knows what options are available and which ones may be appropriate for you is invaluable. Choose a financial professional to work with who understands your needs and can connect you to the appropriate resources.

You will want to **work with a retirement planning professional** who has experience in:

- IRA/401(k) rollovers
- Asset protection

- Income planning
- Wealth management
- Long-term care solutions
- Insurance
- Estate planning
- Wealth transfer strategies

The information you've read in the introduction to this book may have already changed your view on retirement. The information in the ensuing chapters can change your approach to life in retirement by giving you confidence, knowledge, and most importantly, *control* over your retirement.

This book will address your entire financial situation from four perspectives:

- Income longevity and replacement
- Asset accumulation and preservation
- Taxes
- Legacy / Distribution

Let's read on and perhaps you'll find the cracks in your nest egg.

1

ORGANIZING YOUR ASSETS

Will we have enough money for retirement?

Will your Social Security benefit, savings and other retirement assets be enough? If you're like Jack and Beverly, you have Unprotected Money. When the couple turned 60 years old, they started thinking about what their lives would be like in the next 10 years. When would they retire? What would their retirement look like? How much money did they have?

They could both count on Social Security benefits, but neither one really knew how much their monthly checks would be, or when to file for them. Jack had a modest pension that he could begin collecting at age 67. He had always hoped to retire before that age. Beverly had a 401(k), but she wasn't exactly sure how it worked, how she could draw money from it and how much income it would provide once she retired.

While Jack and Beverly may sound like they're totally in the dark about their retirement, the truth is there are a lot of people just like them. They know retirement is coming and know they have some assets to rely on, but they aren't sure how it will all come together to provide them with retirement income.

You spend your entire working life hoping what you put into your retirement accounts will help you live comfortably once you clock out of the workforce for good. The key word in that sentiment and the word that can make retirement feel like a looming problem instead of a rewarding life stage, is ***hope***. You hope you'll have enough money.

Leaving your retirement up to chance is inadvisable by nearly any standard, yet millions of people find themselves *hoping* instead of planning for a happy ending. With information, tools and professional guidance, creating a successful retirement plan can put you in control of your financial management.

While you may have built up a 401(k), an IRA, and Social Security benefits, do you know what your financial picture really looks like?

Structuring assets to create an income-generating retirement requires a different approach than earning income via the workforce. Saving money for retirement, which is what you have spent your life doing, and *planning* your retirement are two different things. Both are important. Earning and saving money is different from creating a financial strategy that accounts for your income needs in retirement. Add the complexities of taxes, required minimum distributions (RMDs) from IRAs, and legacy planning, and you can begin to see why happy endings require more than hope. All retirees need a focused and well-executed plan.

Now that you recognize there's more to saving and planning for retirement than filing for your Social Security benefits and drawing income from your 401(k), you can begin to **create a strategy for your retirement** that can have a significant impact on your financial landscape after you stop drawing a paycheck. Understanding how to manage your assets entails risk management, risk diversification, tax planning and income planning preparation throughout your life stages. These strategies can help you leverage more from the hard-earned dollars for your retirement.

NEW IDEAS FOR RETIREMENT

Advice about what to do with money has been around as long as money has existed. Hindsight allows us to see which advice was good and which advice didn't cut the mustard. Some sources of advice have been around for a very long time. While there are some basic investment concepts that have stood the test of time, most strategies that work adapt to changing conditions in the market, in the economy and the world, as well as changes in your personal circumstances.

The reality is that investment strategies and savings plans that worked in the past have encountered challenging new circumstances that have turned them on their heads. The Great Recession of the early 2000's highlighted how old investment ideas were not only ineffective but incredibly destructive to the retirement plans of millions of Americans. The dawn of an entirely restructured health care system brings with it new options and challenges that will undoubtedly change the way insurance companies provide investment products and services.

Perhaps the most important lessons investors learned from the Great Recession is that not understanding where your money is invested (and the potential risks of those investments) can work against you, your plans for retirement and your legacy. Saving and investing money isn't enough to truly get the most out of it. You must create a better plan to manage your assets.

Essentially, managing your money and your investments is an ongoing process that requires customization and adaptation to a changing world. Make no mistake; the world is always changing. What worked for your parents or even your grandparents was probably good advice back then. Those planning for or already in retirement need new ideas and professional guidance.

UNPROTECTED VS. PROTECTED MONEY

Let's take a look at some of the basic truths about money as it relates to saving for retirement.

There are essentially two kinds of money: *Unprotected* and *Protected*. Everyone can divide their money into these two categories. Some have more of one kind than the other. The goal isn't to eliminate one kind of money but to balance them as you approach retirement.

Unprotected Money is money that is at risk. It fluctuates with the market. It has no minimum guarantee. It is subject to investor activity, stock prices, market trends, buying trends, etc. You get the picture. This money is exposed to more risk but also has the potential for more reward. Because the market is subject to change, you can't really be sure what the value of your investments will be worth in the future. You can't really *rely* on it at all. For this reason, we refer to it as Unprotected Money. This doesn't mean you shouldn't have some money invested in the market, but it would be dangerous to assume you can know what it will be worth in the future.

Unprotected Money is an important element of a retirement plan, especially in the early stages of planning when you can trade volatility for potential returns, and when a longer investment timeframe is available to you. In the long run, time can smooth out the ups and downs of money exposed to the market. Working with a professional and leveraging a long-term investment strategy has the potential to create rewarding returns from Unprotected Money.

Protected Money, on the other hand, is far less exposed when compared to Unprotected Money. Protected Money is made up of dependable, low-risk or no-risk money, and investments that you can count on. Social Security is one of the most common forms of Protected Money. Income you draw or will draw from Social Security is guaranteed. You have paid into Social Security your entire career, and you can rely on that money during your retirement. Unlike the market, rates of growth for Protected Money are dependent on 10-year treasury rates. The 10-year treasury, or

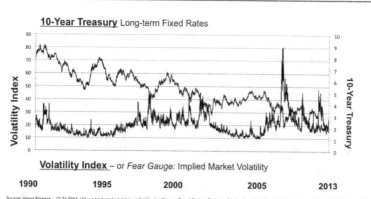

10-Year Treasury Long-term Fixed Rates

Volatility Index – or *Fear Gauge:* Implied Market Volatility

Source: Yahoo Finance – 12-31-2013. VIX is a trademarked ticker symbol for the Chicago Board Options Exchange Market Volatility Index, a popular measure of the implied volatility of S&P 500 index options. Often referred to as the fear index or the fear gauge, it represents one measure of the market's expectation of stock market volatility over the next 30 day period. (wikipedia.com) The CBOE 10-year Treasury Note (TNX) is based on 10 times the yield-to-maturity on the most recently auctioned 10-year Treasury note. Past performance does not guarantee future results. Some illustrations may show how a market index has performed. An investor cannot invest in an index, although there are some investments designed to mirror index performance. Past performance is not a guarantee of future results.

The VIX, or volatility index, of the market represents expected market volatility. When the VIX drops, economic experts expect less volatility. When the VIX rises, more volatility is expected.

1. *VIX is a trademarked ticker symbol for the Chicago Board Options Exchange (CBOE) Market Volatility Index, a popular measure of the implied volatility of S&P 500 index options. Often referred to as the fear index or the fear gauge, it represents one measure of the market's expectation of stock market volatility over the next 30 day period. (wikipedia.com)*

2. *The CBOE 10-Year Treasury Note (TNX) is based on 10 times the yield-to-maturity on the most recently auctioned 10-year Treasury note.*

TNX, is commonly considered to represent a very secure and safe place for your money, hence Protected Money. The 10-year treasury drives key rates for things such as mortgage rates or CD rates. Protected Money may not be as exciting as Unprotected Money, but it is safer. You can be fairly sure you will have it in the future.

Knowing the difference between Unprotected and Protected Money is an important step towards a successful retirement plan. People who are 55 or older and who are looking ahead to retirement should be relying on more Protected Money than Unprotected Money.

Ideally, the rates of return on Unprotected and Protected Money would have an overlapping area that provides an acceptable rate of risk for both types of money. In the early 1990s, interest rates were high and market volatility was low. At that time, you could invest in either Unprotected or Protected Money options because the rates of return were similar from both Protected and Unprotected investments, and you were likely to be fairly successful with a wide range of investment options. At that time, you could expose yourself to an acceptable amount of risk or an acceptable fixed rate. Basically, it was difficult to make a mistake during that time period. Today, you don't have those options. Market volatility is at all-time highs while interest rates are at all-time lows. They are so far apart from each other that it is hard to know what to do with your money.

Yesterday's investment rules may not work today. Not only could they hamper achieving your goals, they may actually harm your financial situation. We are currently in a period when the rates for Protected Money options are at historic lows, and the volatility of Unprotected Money is higher than ever. There is no overlapping acceptable rate, making both options less than ideal. *Because of this uncertain financial landscape, wise investment strategies are more important now than ever.*

This unique situation requires fresh ideas and investment tools that haven't been implemented in the past. Investing the way your parents did years ago will not pay off. The majority of investment ideas used by financial professionals in the 1990s aren't applicable in today's markets. Today, you need a better plan.

HOW MUCH RISK ARE YOU EXPOSED TO?

Many investors don't know how much risk they are exposed to. It is helpful to organize your assets so you can have a clear understanding of how much of your money is at risk and how much is in safer investments. This process starts with listing all your assets.

Let's take a look at the two kinds of money:

Unprotected Money is, as the name indicates, money that you *hope* will be there when you need it. Unprotected Money represents taking more risk for potentially higher gains. Examples of Unprotected Money include:
- Stock market funds, including index funds
- Mutual funds
- Variable annuities
- REITS

Protected Money is money that you know you can count on. It is safer money that isn't exposed to the level of volatility as the asset types noted above. You can more confidently count on having this money when you need it. Examples of Protected Money are:
- Government backed bonds
- Savings and checking accounts
- Fixed or index annuities
- CDs
- Treasuries
- Money market accounts

» *Ben had a modest brokerage account that he added to when he could. When he changed jobs a couple years ago, at age 58, Ben transferred his 401(k) assets into an IRA. Just a few years from retirement, he is now beginning to realize that nearly every dollar he has saved for retirement is subject to market risk.*

Intuitively, he knows that the time has come to shift some assets to an alternative that is safer, but how much is the right amount?

KNOW YOUR RISK LEVEL

Determining the amount of risk that is right for you is dependent on a number of variables. You need to feel comfortable with where and how you are investing your money, and your financial professional is obligated to help you make decisions that put your money in places that fit your desired level of risk.

Your retirement needs to first accommodate your day-to-day income needs. How much money do you need to maintain your lifestyle? When do you need it?

Managing your risk by having a balance of Unprotected Money vs. Protected Money is a good start that will put you ahead of the curve. But how much Protected Money is enough to secure your income needs during retirement, and how much Unprotected Money is enough to allow you to continue to benefit from an improving market?

In short, how do you know how much risk you should be exposed to in your investments?

While there is no single approach to investment risk advice that is universally applicable to everyone, there are some helpful guidelines. One of the most useful is called *The Rule of 100*.

The average investor needs to accumulate assets to create a retirement plan that provides income during retirement and also allows for legacy planning. To accomplish this, they need to balance the amount of risk to which they are exposed. Risk is required because, while Protected Money is safer, more reliable and more dependable, it doesn't grow very fast, if at all. Today's historically low interest rates barely break even with current inflation. Unprotected Money, while less dependable, has more potential for growth. Unprotected Money can eventually become Protected Money once you move it to an investment with lower risk. Everyone's risk diversification will be different depending on their goals, age and their existing assets.

How do you decide how much risk your assets should be exposed to? Where do you begin? Luckily, there's a guideline you can use to start making decisions about risk management. It's called the Rule of 100.

THE RULE OF 100

This is a general rule that helps shape asset diversification* for the average investor. The rule states that the number 100 minus an investor's age equals the amount of assets they should have exposed to risk.

The Rule of 100: 100 - (your age) = the percentage of your assets that should be exposed to risk.

For example, if you are a 30-year-old investor, the Rule of 100 would indicate that you should be focusing on investing primarily in the market and taking on a substantial amount of risk in your portfolio. The Rule of 100 suggests that 70 percent of your investments should be exposed to risk.

Asset Diversification disclosure – Diversification and asset allocation does not assure or guarantee better performance and cannot eliminate the risk of investment loss. Before investing, you should carefully read the applicable volatility disclosure for each of the underlying funds, which can be found in the current prospectus.

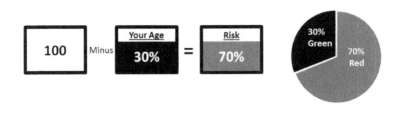

Now, not every 30-year-old should have exactly 70 percent of their assets in mutual funds and stocks. The Rule of 100 is based on your chronological age, not your "financial age," which could vary based on your investment experience, your aversion or acceptance of risk and other factors. While this rule isn't an ironclad solution to anyone's finances, it's a pretty good place to start. Once you've taken the time to look at your assets with a professional to determine your risk exposure, you can use the Rule of 100 to make changes that put you in a more stable investment position—one that reflects your comfort level.

Perhaps when you were age 30 and starting your career, like in the example above, it made sense to have 70 percent of your money in the market: you had time on your side. You had plenty of time to save more money, work more and recover from a downturn in the market. Retirement was years away, and your earning power was increasing. And indeed, younger investors should take on more risk for exactly those reasons. The potential reward of long-term involvement in the market outweighs the risk of investing when you are young.

Risk tolerance generally lessens as you get older, however. If you are 40 years old and lose 30 percent of your portfolio in a market downturn this year, you have 20 or 30 years to recover it. If you are 68 years old, you have five to 10 years, or less, to make the same recovery. That changes your whole retirement perspective. At age 68, it's likely that you simply aren't as interested in suffering through a tough stock market. There is less time to recover from downturns, and the stakes are higher. The money you have saved is money you will soon need to provide you with income, or is money that you already need to meet your income demands. Much of the flexibility that comes with investing earlier in life is related to *compounding*. Compounded earnings can be incredibly powerful over time. The longer your money has time to compound, the greater your wealth will be. This is what most people talk about when they refer to putting their money to work. This is also why the Rule of 100 favors risk for the young. If you start investing when you are young, you can invest smaller amounts of money in a more aggressive manner because you have the potential to make a profit in a rising market and you can harness the power of compounded earnings. When you are 40, 50 or 60 years old, that potential becomes less and less and you are forced to invest more money at lower amounts of risk to realize the same returns.

You risk not having a recovery period the older you get, so you should have fewer of your assets at risk in volatile investments. You should adopt the Rule of 100 to protect your assets and ensure that they will provide the income you need in retirement. Let's look at another example that illustrates how the Rule of 100 becomes more critical as you age. An 80-year-old investor who is retired and is relying on retirement assets for income, for example, needs to depend on a solid amount of Protected Money. The Rule of 100 says an 80-year-old investor should have a maximum of 20 percent of his or her assets at risk. Depending on the investor's financial position, less risk exposure may be required. You are the only person who can make this kind of determination, but the Rule of 100 can help. Everyone has their own level of comfort. Your Rule of 100 results will be based on your values and attitudes as well as your comfort with risk.

The Rule of 100 can apply to overall financial management and to specific investment products that you own as well. Take the 401(k) for example. Many people have them, but not many people understand how their money is allocated within their 401(k). An employer may have someone who comes in once a year and explains the models and options that employees can choose from, but that's as much guidance as most 401(k) holders get. Many 401(k) options include target date funds that change their risk exposure over time, essentially following a form of the Rule of 100. Selecting one of these options can often be a good move for employees because they shift your risk as you age, securing more Protected Money when you need it.

A financial professional can look at your assets with you and discuss alternatives to optimize your balance between Protected and Unprotected Money.

WHAT IS YOUR RISK LEVEL?

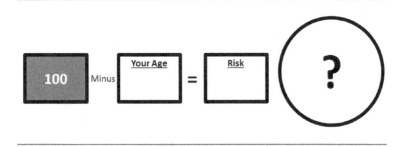

CHAPTER 1 RECAP //

- There is money you <u>hope</u> you'll have in the future, and there's money you <u>know</u> you'll have in the future.
- Organizing your assets starts with making a list. You can then understand how each asset is balanced for risk.
- Your exposure to risk is ultimately determined by you.
- Use the Rule of 100 as a general guiding principle when determining how much risk your retirement investments should be exposed to (100 - [your age] = [percentage of your investments that can comfortably be exposed to risk]). In other words, take your age, add a percent sign after it, and that is the amount of your portfolio that should be in safe, guaranteed, zero risk accounts.

2

THE COLOR OF MONEY

Going a step further, we can organize the types of investments and assets you have into a helpful visual schematic.

It can be helpful to assign colors to the different kinds of money and their level of risk. For example, call Protected Money (which is safer and more dependable) green. Unprotected Money (which is exposed to risk and fluctuates with the market) we will call red. A financial professional can help you better understand the color of the money in your investment portfolio.

Visually organizing your assets is an important and powerful way to get a clear picture of what kind of money you have, where it is and how you can best use it in the future. This process is as simple as listing your assets and assigning them a color based on their status as Protected or Unprotected Money. Work with your financial professional to create a comprehensive inventory of your assets to understand what you are working with before making any decisions. This may be the first time you have ever sat down and sorted out all of your assets, allowing you to see how much money you have at risk in the market. Comparing the color of your investments will give you an idea of how near or far you are from adhering to the Rule of 100.

Over the course of your lifetime, it is likely that you have acquired a variety of assets. Liquid assets can range from money that you have in a savings account or a 401(k), to a pension or an IRA. You have earned money and have made financial decisions based on the best information you had at the time. When viewed as a whole, however, you might not have an overall strategy for the management of your assets. As we have seen, it's more important than ever to know which of your assets are at risk. High market volatility and low treasury rates make for challenging financial topography. Navigating this financial landscape starts with asset management that focuses on your specific needs and objectives.

Even if you feel that you have plenty of money in your 401(k) or IRA, not knowing how much *risk* those investments are exposed to can cause you major financial suffering. Take the market crash of 2008 for example. In 2008, the average investor lost 30 percent of their 401(k). If more people had shifted their investments away from risk as they neared retirement age (i.e. the Rule of 100), they may have reduced their losses.

When using the Rule of 100 to calculate your level of risk, your financial age might be different from your chronological age, however. The way you organize your assets depends on your goals and your level of comfort with risk. Whatever you determine the appropriate amount of risk to take, you should organize your portfolio to reflect your goals. If you have more Red Money than Green Money, in particular, you will need to make decisions about how to invest. You can work with a financial professional to find appropriate Protected Money options for your situation.

The next step is to know the right amount and ratio of Green and Red Money for you at your stage of retirement planning.

Investing heavily in Red Money and gambling all of your assets on the market is incredibly risky no matter where you fall within the Rule of 100. Money in the market can't be depended on to generate income, and a plan that leans too heavily on Red Money can easily fail, especially when investment decisions are influenced by emotional reactions to market downturns and recoveries. Not only is this an unwise plan, it can be incredibly stressful to an investor who is gambling everything on stocks and mutual funds.

But a plan that uses too much Green Money avoids all volatility and can also fail. Why? Investing all of your money in Certificates of Deposit (CDs), savings accounts, money markets and other low return accounts may provide interest and income, but that likely won't be enough to keep pace with inflation. If you focus exclusively on income from Green Money and avoid owning any stocks or mutual funds in your portfolio, you won't be able to leverage the potential for long-term growth your portfolio needs to stay healthy and productive. The Rule of 100 can help you determine how much of your money should be invested in the market to anticipate your future needs.

Green Money becomes much more important as you age. While you want to reduce the amount of Red Money you have and to transition it to Green Money, you don't necessarily need all of it to generate income for you right away. Taking a closer look at Green Money, you will see there are two different types.

TYPES OF GREEN MONEY:
NEED NOW AND NEED LATER

Money that you need to depend on for income is Green Money. Once you have filled the income gap at the beginning of your retirement, you may have money left over.

There are two types of Green Money: money used for immediate income and money used for accumulation to meet your income needs in five, 10 or 20 years. Money needed for income is Need Now Money. It is money you need to meet your basic needs, pay your bills, pay your mortgage (if you have one) and the costs associated with maintaining your lifestyle. Money used for accumulation is Need Later Money. It's money that you don't need now but will rely upon in the future. It's still Green Money because you will rely on it later for income and will need to count on it being accessible. Need Later Money represents income your assets will need to generate for future use. When planning your retirement, it is vital to decide how much of your assets to structure for income and how much to set aside to create Need Later Money.

You must figure out if your income and accumulation needs are met. Your Need Now and Need Later Money are top priorities. Need Now Money, in particular, will dictate what your options for future needs are.

OPTIMIZING RISK AND FINDING THE RIGHT BALANCE

Determining the amount of risk that is right for you depends on your specific situation. It starts by examining your financial position.

The Rule of 100 is a useful way to begin to determine the right amount of risk for you. Use it as a starting point to figure out where your money should be. If you're a 50-year-old investor, the Rule of 100 suggests that you have 50 percent Green Money and 50 percent Red Money. Many 50-year-olds are more risk tolerant. There are many reasons why someone might be more risk tolerant, not the least of which is feeling young! Experienced investors, people who feel they need to gamble for a higher return, or people who have met their retirement income goals and are looking for additional ways to accumulate wealth are all candidates for investment strategies that incorporate higher levels of risk. In the end, it comes down to your personal tolerance for risk. How much are you willing to lose?

Consulting with a financial professional is often the wisest approach to calculating your risk level. A professional can help determine your risk tolerance by getting to know you, asking questions to determine your comfort level with different types of risk. Here's a typical scenario a financial professional might pose to you:

"You have $100,000 saved that you would like to invest in the market. There is an investment product that could turn your $100,000 into $120,000. That same option, however, has the potential of losing you up to $30,000, leaving you with $70,000."

Is that a scenario that you are willing to enter into? Or are you more comfortable with this one:

"You could turn your $100,000 into $110,000, but have the potential of losing $15,000, leaving you with $85,000."

Your answer to these and others types of questions will help a financial professional determine what level of risk is right for you. They can then offer you investment strategies and management plans that reflect your financial age.

10 INVESTING SCAMS: BEWARE

Leveraging your Red Money wisely can provide you with returns, and help increase the value of assets that you plan to use for income at a later date. Unfortunately, there's always someone ready to empty the pockets of an investor who's overly eager for unrealistic returns. Here are some of the most prevalent schemes as published by www.bankrate.com:

1. PONZI SCHEMES The late Charles Ponzi invented this scheme in the early 1900s. By the time he was through, he had conned more than $10 million from investors, promising unrealistic 40 percent returns. Since then, his scam has been copied by countless people. Here's how it works: someone promises an investor high returns and then turns around and uses their money to pay previous investors.

2. SENIOR INVESTMENT FRAUD With rising healthcare costs and record-low investment rates, coupled with increased life expectancies, many seniors have become targets for investment fraud by con artists. Scams range from Ponzi schemes and unregistered securities to promissory notes and charitable gift annuities.

3. PROMISSORY NOTES These short-term debt instruments are often sold by independent insurance agents, and are issued by either independent or nonexistent companies.

4. UNSCRUPULOUS STOCKBROKERS In an effort to disguise falling share prices and losses on investments, some less than honest stockbrokers may resort to fraud. Many suspicious investors have discovered that financial advisers have been charging them unexplained fees, making unauthorized trades, and undertaking a host of other irregular activities.

5. AFFINITY FRAUD Leveraging religious or ethnic identity as a way to gain the trust of investors, some agents of fraud will then use techniques like "gifting" programs at churches or foreign exchange scams in order to steal money from investors.

6. UNLICENSED INDIVIDUALS SELLING SECURITIES Using the promise of high commissions, many scam artists encourage independent insurance agents to sell risky investments that they don't know about or understand. The person behind the scam directs agents to make unlicensed sales that promise a high rate or returns with minimal risk. If you are approached by an independent agent making promises that seem too good to be true, make sure to call your state's securities regulator to find out if they are a licensed salesperson. Inquire whether the investment is registered as well. If the answer is yes, you can approach the product with more confidence, but be very skeptical as you learn more about the opportunity.

7. "PRIME BANK" SCHEMES Double and triple digit returns promised by con artists who have access to the elite banks of the world are known as prime bank schemes. The Federal Reserve has pointed out that elite, exclusive investment programs like this don't exist, but many conspiracy theorists think otherwise.

8. INTERNET FRAUD Many of the investment scams found on the Internet today are recycled forms of existing ones. The difference is that online marketing tools and websites can reach millions more people and can often look legitimate.

9. MUTUAL FUND BUSINESS PRACTICES Some recent scandals in the mutual fund market have made national news, attracting the attention of investors and investigators.

10. VARIABLE ANNUITIES (EVEN THOSE WITH WELL KNOWN, REPUTABLE INSURANCE COMPANIES) While there are many good annuity products available to investors, some <u>variable</u> annuities have come under criticism for their omission of disclosure about surrender charges and steep sales commissions. The risk inherent to <u>variable</u> annuities <u>may not be suitable</u> for retired people. Consider other annuity options.

THE NUMBERS DON'T LIE

When the rubber meets the road, the numbers dictate your options. Your risk tolerance is an important indicator of what kinds of investments you should consider, but if the returns from those investments don't meet your retirement goals, your income needs will likely not be met. For example, if the level of risk you are comfortable with can only guarantee a 4 percent return on your investments and you need to realize an 8 percent return, your income needs aren't going to be met when you need to rely on your investments for retirement income. A professional may encourage you to be more aggressive with your investment strategy by taking on more risk in order to give you the potential of earning a greater return. If taking more risk isn't an option that you are comfortable with, then the discussion will turn to how you can earn more money or spend less in order to align your needs with your resources more closely.

How are you going to structure your income flow during retirement? The answer to this question dictates how you determine your risk tolerance. If the numbers indicate you need to be more aggressive with your investing, or need to modify your lifestyle, it becomes a choice you need to make.

WORKING WITH A RETIREMENT PLANNING FINANCIAL PROFESSIONAL

Take a moment to think about your income goals:

What is your lifestyle today? Would you like to maintain it into retirement? Are you meeting your needs? Are you happy with your lifestyle? What do you really *need* to live on when you retire?

Some people will have the luxury of maintaining or improving their lifestyle, while others may have to make decisions about what they need versus what they want during their retirement.

Organizing your assets, understanding the color of your money, and creating an income and accumulation plan for retirement can quickly become an overwhelming task. The fact of the matter is that financial professionals build their careers around understanding the different variables affecting retirement financing.

Working with a Registered Investment Advisor means working with a professional who is legally obligated to help you make financial decisions that are in your best interest and fall within your comfort zone. Taking steps toward creating a retirement plan is nothing to take lightly. By leveraging tax strategies, properly organizing your assets, and accumulating helpful financial products that help you meet your income and accumulation needs, you are more likely to meet your goals. You might have a million dollars socked away in a savings account, but your neighbor, who has $300,000 in a diverse investment portfolio that is tailored to their needs, may end up enjoying a better retirement lifestyle. Why? They had more than a good work ethic and a penchant for saving. They had a planful approach to retirement asset allocation.

IMPROVING BY CHANGING YOUR MINDSET

Your investment situation is as unique as you are. Decisions you have made along the way to retirement are a reflection of your choices. The following points are intended to give you perspective on how your portfolio can be improved by the way you approach investing.

You are 100 percent responsible for all of your successes and failures. You control everything: your accountant, your lawyer, your financial professional, where you invest and what you invest in. When things fail, don't blame anyone but yourself. You are where you are because of your decisions. You can always change your decisions and change where you are. Improvement does not happen by chance or by continuing what isn't working. Improvement comes with changing your mindset and your decisions. You are responsible for your own success. The only limits are those you impose upon yourself.

Your portfolio is a reflection of you. If you complain about your portfolio or blame it on the stock market or economy, it's really *your* fault. Have you read any books on investing? *The Millionaire Next Door? Missed Fortune 101?* What actions have you taken to stop your losses? When you hear others complain about their portfolio, it's because they didn't plan and gave full control to someone regarding their financial decisions. They complain but they were doomed for failure. You don't have to be that kind of person. You can stop blaming you bank advisor or agent. You chose your advisor and allowed him or her to put you into whatever situation they recommended. You can improve by learning from your past. The more vocal you become, the more successful your investments will be. When you start making better decisions, gather facts not hunches, and put feelings and relationships aside, your financial, estate and tax obligations will improve.

You have to do something to get out of your routine. You cannot improve without change. You cannot keep doing the same thing over and over again and expect different results. If you want better results, you must do things differently. This means nothing more than stepping outside your routine. If there is no meaningful change, there cannot be a meaningful improvement. You have to revisit what you want, your objectives, and what you want to happen.

Not all bankers, advisors, or planners deserve you. You may not be getting the service you deserve: calls not returned, investments diminishing, losses increasing without a plan of action to stop them, etc. If you don't value yourself first and keep your money out of harm's way, who will? If you don't step up and make demands, why should an advisor take you seriously? Does the person you are sitting across from when you go to their office deserve your business?

Set up systems to get organized and monitor your returns weekly. This is something that you should have been doing long ago. If so, would your net worth be different today?

What can you do to improve your focus on your assets? As an investor, you must spend time thinking about your money: improving returns, stopping losses, increasing income, and reducing taxes. Identify exactly what dollar amount you are paying in fees to your broker. You can't stick your head in the sand. Take control. Check your accounts and investments once a week. This will allow you to make improvements sooner and minimize losses.

Consider multiple sources to acquire knowledge and facts. Attend seminars, utilize the internet, watch TV programs, read books, magazines, and newspapers. The more you know, the more you benefit.

Recognize that opportunity is always available. You get what you are looking for, or not looking for. If you are looking for speculation and risk, you'll find it and get it. If you are looking to rebuild your portfolio, beat bank CD and IRA rates, and reduce taxes, you can accomplish it. Look for prosperity and keep an open mind.

Embrace new ways to achieve your goals. You probably have financial concerns that you'd like to improve. It doesn't happen unless you are willing to change what's broken and not working. Change will create new opportunities, help you grow as a person, and put you on a path to improve your investments.

CHAPTER 2 RECAP //

- There are two types of money: Green and Red. Green Money represents assets that are safer and more reliable. Red Money represents assets that are exposed to risk.
- There are two types of Green Money: *Need Now and Need Later*. It is important to structure your investments to provide you with income now and later.
- Working with a Registered Investment Advisor will help you compose a clear and concise inventory of your assets, learn how much they are worth, what rules apply to them, and how they are structured for risk.
- A Registered Investment Advisor can help you structure your investments so as to reflect your risk tolerance.
- Working with an Investment Advisor means working with a professional who is legally obligated to help you make financial decisions that are in your best interest and fall within your comfort zone.
- Your investment situation is as unique as you are.

3

CREATING AN INCOME PLAN

An important aspect of your financial plan is the evaluation of your income needs. Finding the most efficient and beneficial way to address them will have impacts on your lifestyle, your asset accumulation and your legacy planning after you retire. When you have identified your income need, you will know how much to allocate for income and how much to set aside for accumulation.

Every financial strategy for retirement needs to accommodate the day-to-day need for income. The moment your working income ceases and you start living off the money you've set aside for retirement is referred to as the **retirement cliff**. When you begin drawing income from your retirement assets, you have entered the distribution phase of your financial plan. This is when you reach the point of relying on your assets for income. This is where your Green Money comes into play: the safer, more reliable assets that you have accumulated that are designed to provide you with a steady income. On day one of your retirement, you will need a steady and reliable supply of income from your Green Money.

To satisfy your need for daily income you must know *how much you need* and *when you will need it.*

How Much Money Do You Need? This amount will be different for everyone. The general rule of thumb is that a retiree will require 70 to 80 percent of their pre-retirement income to maintain their lifestyle. Once you determine that number, the key becomes matching your income needs with the correct investment strategies, options and tools to satisfy your needs.

When Do You Need Your Money? If you need income to last 10 years, use a tool that creates just that. If you need a lifetime of income, seek a tool that will do that and won't run out.

So how do you figure out how much you need and when you need it? When you take health care costs, potential emergencies, plans for moving or traveling, and other retirement expenses into account, you can really give your calculator a workout. You want to maximize retirement benefits to meet your lifetime income needs. An Investment Advisor can help you answer those questions by working with you to customize an income plan.

COMMON MISTAKES INVESTORS MAKE
- **Investing in bonds in a low interest environment.** When interest rates rise just 2 percent and you cash them in for a better rate, your bond value could lose up to 13 percent. Buy bonds when rates are higher.
- **Too much risk.** Overexposure in the market for older investors may not be good. Be sure to keep a portion out of harm's way. Refer to the Rule of 100.
- **Complacency and Procrastination.** You take care of your car, plan vacations and meet with your accountant. You

should also pay close attention to your money. Getting a fresh perspective from another advisor will help you tremendously.

- **Continuing to accept bad investment advice.** Has the broker responsible for your losses helped you recover them? If not, consider seeking better advice soon.
- **Taking payments instead of a lump sum on company pension and 401(k) plans.** Never give up control of your money when you leave. Roll over your retirement plan to a broker or financial advisor of your choice. By doing a little shopping, you could get a higher monthly income from outside investments and you won't lose your nest egg if your former employer goes bankrupt.
- **Having an outdated (or no) will or trust.** It took a lot of sacrifice to save what you have. Take the steps now to protect it.
- **Taking interest-only income.** It's 100 percent taxable. There are better income strategies that are up to 95 percent tax free. Talk to your financial professional for details.
- **Keeping too much money liquid in low interest, taxable bank accounts.** Your bank will get wealthier, but you won't. Having too much money in banks results in much less growth and unnecessary annual taxes. Have more money for the years ahead, and lower your taxes by using the right, fully insured, safe tax-deferred investments. Only use banks for paying bills and emergency money.
- **Not having long term care, nursing home, assisted living or home health care coverage.** Your nest egg can be easily wiped out. Ask me about other options. There are other strategies besides purchasing long term care insurance to consider.
- **Taking unnecessary taxable income.** Why take so much if you are losing the growth on the invested money and creat-

ing unnecessarily higher tax obligations? Use only what you really need and leave the rest invested.

- **Investing because you are familiar with the company.** You are not buying the company or the bank, you are purchasing an investment. Not all investment products with well known companies are the best choice for you. Know the fine print.
- **Making your estate your beneficiary.** By not designating non-spousal beneficiaries, you can expose your estate to probate and other costly fees.
- **Hanging on to losing investments.** The sooner you switch to a better investment, the quicker you may recover losses and show gains.
- **Letting a broker run free with investment decisions.** Did your broker tell you to "hang in there" when the market dropped? Express your concerns, watch your statements closely, and get more involved. Make sure you approve all changes before they are made.
- Placing IRA required minimum distribution in a taxable bank account. After paying taxes on your RMDs, placing them in a taxable account means you will expose it to more taxation. Reinvest your distribution in a tax deferred annuity, or spend it. Note that earnings in a tax deferred annuity will be taxed upon withdrawal.
- **Not updating low interest fixed annuities or risky and costly variable annuities.** Why sit there with below average rates or with a variable annuity that has costly fees and is losing money? Make a positive change now.
- **Not having an income plan in place that is guaranteed to last as long as you live or to replace lost income when a spouse dies.**
- Not having a strategy in place to distribute money properly to your children. Giving children a lump sum could end up

in a devastating loss of 40 to 60 percent of your investment values, especially if it is IRA money. Consider the Stretch IRA instead.

WHAT EXPERIENCED INVESTORS HAVE LEARNED

Over the years, investors have made mistakes with their investment choices. The following are "Pearls of Wisdom" we have gleaned from more than 1500 survey responses from senior investors:

- A big mistake is taking investment advice from people who are not qualified to give it. Get financial advice regarding your retirement only from professionals who devote their lives to creating successful retirement plans.
- The biggest mistakes you can make with your money are neglect, procrastination and being complacent. Many people need motivation. Those that accept change will do better.
- You make money by using your brains and lose it by listening to your heart. Cut your losses quickly on ventures where you have been wrong.
- The true secret of successful investing is knowing which investments to avoid.
- Every year evaluate and reset your goals.
- Markets change continuously and so must you. What worked in the past may very well not work this year. Accept change in your strategy.
- Find a company that focuses on what matters to you, not what they *must* or *want to* sell you.
- You can't be sentimental about your investments and make money from them.
- If you aren't clever enough at selling stocks, you'll soon see your profits turn into losses. When in doubt, get out.
- Love your spouse and your children, but don't love your stocks. There is no guarantee they will be good to you in

the future. The stock doesn't know you own it. It's a piece of paper.
- Conservative investors sleep well.
- Hire an advisor who does the right thing and does things right.
- The individual who acts now, not later, is the one who ends up with more money.
- None of the secrets of success work unless you get going.
- Financial prosperity is the result of good planning.

As we determined earlier in Chapter 1, the most important thing you need to do as you create an income plan is to avoid too much exposure to risk. You can start by meeting with an Investment Advisor to organize your assets. Get your Green Money and Red Money in order and balanced to meet your needs. If the market goes down 18 percent this afternoon, you don't want that to come out of what you're relying on for next year's income. Hot on the heels of securing your Green Money, it's time to structure those Green Money assets so they can generate income for you. Ultimately, you have to take care of your monthly income needs to pay the bills.

The Big Kahuna of Green Money is your Social Security benefit, which we will cover in the next chapter.

CHAPTER 3 RECAP //
- The foundation of a retirement strategy depends on knowing how much money you need and when you need it.

4

UNDERSTANDING
SOCIAL SECURITY

One kind of Green Money that most Americans rely on for income when they retire is Social Security. If you're like most Americans, Social Security is or will be an important part of your retirement income and one that you should know how to properly manage. As a first step in creating your income plan, a financial professional will take a look at your Social Security benefit options. Social Security is the foundation of income planning for anyone who is about to retire and is a reliable source of Green Money in your overall income plan.

> » *Mary had worked full-time nearly her entire adult life and was looking forward to enjoying retirement with her husband, kids and grandkids. When she turned 62, she decided*

to take advantage of her Social Security benefits as soon as they became available.

A couple of years later, she was organizing some of the paperwork in her home office. She came across an old Social Security statement, and remembered the feeling of filing and beginning a new phase in her life.

However, as she looked over the statement, she realized in retrospect that she might have been better off waiting to file for benefits. She had saved enough to wait for benefits, and if she had, her monthly benefit could have been quite a bit more.

When she was in the process of retiring, there were so many other decisions to make. It seemed very straightforward to file right away. She made a note to call the Social Security Administration to see if it was possible to change her monthly benefit to the larger amount.

Here are some facts that illustrate how Americans currently use Social Security:

- Nearly 90 percent of Americans age 65 and older receive Social Security benefits.*
- Social Security provides about 39 percent of the income of the elderly.*
- Claiming Social Security benefits at the wrong time can reduce your monthly benefit by up to 65 percent.**
- In 2013, 36 percent of men and 40 percent of women claimed Social Security benefits at age 62.***

---

* *http://www.ssa.gov/pressoffice/basicfact.htm*

** *https://www.ssa.gov/planners/retire/retirechart.html*

*** *Trends in Social Security Claiming, Alicia H Munnell and Anqi Chen, Center for Retirement Research, May 2015. http://crr.bc.edu/wp-content/uploads/2015/05/IB_15-8.pdf*

- In 2013, more than a third of workers claimed Social Security benefits as soon they became eligible.*
- In 2015, the average monthly Social Security benefit was $1,328. The maximum benefit for 2015 was $2,663. The $1,335 monthly benefit reduction between the average and the maximum is applied for life.**

There are many aspects of Social Security that are well known and others that aren't. When it comes time for you to cash in on your Social Security benefit, you will have many options and choices. Social Security is a massive government program that manages retirement benefits for millions of people. Experts spend their entire careers understanding and analyzing it. Luckily, you don't have to understand all of the intricacies of Social Security to maximize its advantages.

You simply need to know the best way to manage your Social Security benefit. You need to know exactly what to do to get the most from your Social Security benefit and when to do it. Taking the time to create a roadmap for your Social Security strategy will help ensure that you are able to exact your maximum benefit and efficiently coordinate it with the rest of your retirement plan.

There are many aspects of Social Security that you have no control over. You don't control how much you put into it, and you don't control what it's invested in or how the government manages it. However, you do control when and how you file for benefits. The real question about Social Security that you need to answer is, "When should I start taking Social Security?" While this is the all-important question, there are a couple of key pieces of information you need to track down first.

---

* *Trends in Social Security Claiming, Alicia H Munnell and Anqi Chen, Center for Retirement Research, May 2015. http://crr.bc.edu/wp-content/uploads/2015/05/IB_15-8.pdf*

** *https://www.ssa.gov/news/press/factsheets/colafacts2015.html*

Before we get into a few calculations and strategies that can make all the difference, let's start by covering the basic information about Social Security which should give you an idea of where you stand. Just as the foundation of a house creates the stable platform for the rest of the framework to rest upon, your Social Security benefit is an important part of your overall retirement plan. The purpose of the information that follows is not to give an exhaustive explanation of how Social Security works, but to give you some tools and questions to start understanding how Social Security affects your retirement and how you can prepare for it.

Let's start with eligibility.

Eligibility. Understanding how and when you are eligible for Social Security benefits will help clarify what to expect when the time comes to claim them.

To receive retirement benefits from Social Security, you must earn eligibility. In almost all cases, Americans born after 1929 must earn 40 quarters of credit to be eligible to draw their Social Security retirement benefit. In 2015, a Social Security credit represents $1,220 earned in a calendar quarter. The number changes as it is indexed each year, but not drastically. In 2014, a credit represented $1,200. Four quarters of credit is the maximum number that can be earned each year. In 2015, an American would have had to earn at least $4,880 to accumulate four credits. In order to qualify for retirement benefits, you must have earned a minimum number of credits. Additionally, if you are at least 62 years old and have been married to a recipient of Social Security benefits for at least 12 months, you can choose to receive Spousal Benefits. Although 40 is the minimum number of credits required to begin drawing benefits, it is important to know that once you claim your Social Security benefit, there is no going back. Although there may be cost of living adjustments made, you are locked into that base benefit amount forever.

Primary Insurance Amount. You can think of your Primary Insurance Amount (PIA) like a ripening fruit. It represents the amount of your Social Security benefit at your Full Retirement Age (FRA). Your benefit becomes fully ripe at your FRA, and will neither reduce nor increase due to early or delayed retirement options. If you opt to take benefits before your FRA, however, your monthly benefit will be less than your PIA. You will essentially be picking an unripened fruit. On the one hand, waiting until after your FRA to access your benefits will increase your benefit beyond your PIA. On the other hand, you don't want the fruit to overripen, because every month you wait is one less check you get from the government.

Full Retirement Age. Your FRA is an important figure for anyone who is planning to rely on Social Security benefits in their retirement. Depending on when you were born, there is a specific age at which you will attain FRA. Your FRA is dictated by your year of birth and is the age at which you can begin receiving your full monthly benefit. Your FRA is important because it is half of the equation used to calculate your Social Security benefit. The other half of the equation is based on when you start taking benefits.

When Social Security was initially set up, the FRA was age 65, and it still is for people born before 1938. But as time has passed, the age for receiving full retirement benefits has increased. If you were born between 1938 and 1960, your full retirement age is somewhere on a sliding scale between 65 and 67. Anyone born in 1960 or later will now have to wait until age 67 for full benefits. Increasing the FRA has helped the government reduce the cost of the Social Security program, which paid out almost $870 billion to beneficiaries in 2015!*

---

* *https://www.ssa.gov/news/press/basicfact.html*

While you can begin collecting benefits as early as age 62, the amount you receive as a monthly benefit will be less than it would be if you wait until you reach or surpass your FRA. It is important to note that if you file for your Social Security benefit before your FRA, the reduction to your monthly benefit will remain in place for the rest of your life. You can also delay receiving benefits up to age 70, in which case your benefits will be higher than your PIA for the rest of your life.

- At FRA, 100 percent of PIA is available as a monthly benefit.
- At age 62, your Social Security retirement benefits are available. For each month you take benefits prior to your FRA, however, the monthly amount of your benefit is reduced. *This reduction stays in place for the rest of your life.*
- At age 70, your monthly benefit reaches its maximum. After you turn age 70, your monthly benefit will no longer increase.

Year of Birth	Full Retirement Age
1943-1954	66
1955	66 and 2 months
1956	66 and 4 months
1957	66 and 6 months
1958	66 and 8 months
1959	66 and 10 months
1960 or later	age 67*

---

* *http://www.ssa.gov/OACT/progdata/nra.html*

ROLLING UP YOUR SOCIAL SECURITY

Your Social Security income "rolls up" the longer you wait to claim it. Your monthly benefit will continue to increase until you turn 70 years old. Even though Social Security is the foundation of most people's retirement, many Americans feel that they don't have control over how or when they receive their benefits. The truth is that every dollar you increase your Social Security income by means less money you will have to spend from your nest egg to meet your retirement income needs, but many retirees do not take advantage of this fact. For many people, creating their Social Security strategy is the most important decision they can make to positively impact their retirement. *The difference between the best and worst Social Security decision can be tens of thousands of dollars over a lifetime of benefits.*

Deciding NOW or LATER: Following the above logic, it makes sense to wait as long as you can to begin receiving your Social Security benefit. However, the answer isn't always that simple. Not everyone has the option of waiting. Many people need to rely on Social Security on day one of their retirement. Some might need the income. Others might be in poor health and don't feel they will live long enough to make waiting until their FRA worthwhile for themselves or their families. It is also possible, however, that the majority of folks taking an early benefit at age 62 are simply under-informed about Social Security. Perhaps they make this major decision based on rumors and emotion.

File Immediately if You:
- Find your job is unbearable.
- Are willing to sacrifice retirement income.
- Are not healthy and need a reliable source of income.

Consider Delaying Your Benefit if You:
- Want to maximize your retirement income.
- Want to increase retirement benefits for your spouse.
- Are still working and like it.
- Are healthy and willing / able to wait to file.

So if you decide to wait, how long should you wait? Lots of people can put it off for a few years, but not everyone can wait until they are 70 years old. Your individual circumstances may be able to help you determine when you should begin taking Social Security. If you do the math, you will quickly see that between ages 62 and 70, there are 96 months in which you can file for your Social Security benefit. If you take into account those 96 months and the 96 months your spouse could also file for Social Security, and the number of different strategies for structuring your benefit, you can easily end up with more than 20,000 different scenarios. It's safe to say this isn't the kind of math that most people can easily handle. Each month would result in a different benefit amount. The longer you wait, the higher your monthly benefit amount becomes. Each month you wait, however, is one less month that you receive a Social Security check.

The goal is to maximize your lifetime benefits. That may not always mean waiting until you can get the largest monthly payment. Taking the bigger picture into account, you want to find out how to get the most money out of Social Security over the number of years that you draw from it. Don't underestimate the power of optimizing your benefit: the difference between the BEST and WORST Social Security election can easily be worth thousands of dollars in lifetime benefits. The difference can be very substantial!

If you know that every month you wait, your Social Security benefit goes up a little bit, and you also know that every month you wait, you receive one less benefit check, how do you determine where the sweet spot is that maximizes your benefits over your lifetime? Financial professionals have access to software that will calculate the best year and month for you to file for benefits based on your default life expectancy. You can further customize that information by estimating your life expectancy based on your health, habits and family history. If you can then create an income plan (we'll get into this later in the chapter) that helps you wait until the target date for you to file for Social Security, you can optimize your retirement income strategy to get the most out of your Social Security benefit. How can you calculate your life expectancy? Well, you don't know exactly how long you'll live, but you have a better idea than the government does. They rely on averages to make their calculations. You have much more personal information about your health, lifestyle and family history than they do. You can use that knowledge to game the system and beat all the other people who are making uninformed decisions by filing early for Social Security.

While you can and should educate yourself about how Social Security works, the reality is you don't need to know a lot of general information about Social Security in order to make choices about your retirement. What you do need to know is exactly what to do to maximize your benefit. Because knowing what you need to do has huge impacts on your retirement! For most Americans, Social Security is the foundation of income planning for retirement. Social Security benefits represent about 39 percent of the income of the elderly*. For many people, it can represent the largest portion of their retirement income. Not treating your Social Security benefit as an asset and investment tool can lead to sub-optimization of your largest source of retirement income.

Let's take a look at an example that shows the impact of working with a financial professional to optimize Social Security benefits:

---

* *http://www.socialsecurity.gov/pressoffice/basicfact.htm*

» *George and Mary Bailey are a typical American couple who have worked their whole lives and saved when they could. George is 60 years old, and Mary is 56 years old. They sat down with a financial professional who logged onto the Social Security website to look up their PIAs. George's PIA is $1,900 and Mary's is $900.*

If the Baileys cash in at age 62 and begin taking retirement benefits from Social Security, they will receive an estimated $568,600 in lifetime benefits. That may seem like a lot, but if you divide that amount over 20 years, it averages out to around $28,400 per year. The Baileys are accustomed to a more significant annual income than that. To make up the difference, they will have to rely on alternative retirement income options. They will basically have to depend on a bigger nest egg to provide them with the income they need.

If they wait until their FRA, they will increase their lifetime benefits to an estimated $609,000. This option allows them to achieve their Primary Insurance Amount, which will provide them a $34,200 annual income.

After learning the Baileys' needs and using software to calculate the most optimal time to begin drawing benefits, the Baileys' financial professional determined that the best option for them drastically increases their potential lifetime benefits to $649,000!

By using strategies that their financial professional recommended, they increased their potential lifetime benefits by as much as $80,000. There's no telling how much you could miss out on from your Social Security if you don't take time to create a strategy that calculates your maximum benefit. For the Baileys, the value of maximizing their benefits was the difference between night and day. While this may seem like a special case, it isn't uncommon to find benefit increases of this *magnitude. You'll never know unless you take a look at your own options.*

Despite the importance of knowing when and how to take your Social Security benefit, many of today's retirees and pre-retirees may know little about the mechanics of Social Security and how they can maximize their benefit.

So, to whom should you turn for advice when making this complex decision? Before you pick up the phone and call Uncle Sam, you should know that the Social Security Administration (SSA) representatives are actually prohibited from giving you election advice! Plus, SSA representatives in general are trained to focus on monthly benefit amounts, not the lifetime income for a family.

MAXIMIZING YOUR LIFETIME BENEFIT

As discussed earlier, calculating how to maximize lifetime benefits is more important than waiting until age 70 for your maximum monthly benefit amount. It's about getting the most income during your lifetime. Professional benefit maximization software can target the year and month that it is most beneficial for you to file based on your life expectancy.

The three most common ages that people associate with retirement benefits are 62 (Earliest Eligible Age), 66 (Full Retirement Age), and 70 (age at which monthly maximum benefit is reached). In almost all circumstances, however, none of those three most common ages will give you the maximum lifetime benefit.

Remember, every month you wait to file, the amount of your benefit check goes up, but you also get one less check. You don't know how exactly how long you're going to live, but you have a better idea of your life expectancy than the actuaries at the Social Security Administration who can only work with averages. They can't make calculations based on your specific situation. A professional can run the numbers for you and get the target date that maximizes your potential lifetime benefits. You can't get this information from the SSA, but you can get it from a financial professional.

Types of Social Security Benefits:
- *Retired Worker Benefit.* This is the benefit with which most people are familiar. The Retired Worker Benefit is what most people are talking about when they refer to Social Security. It is your benefit based on your earnings and the amount that you have paid into the system over the span of your career.
- *Spousal Benefit.* This is available to the spouse of someone who is eligible for Retired Worker Benefits.
- *Survivorship Benefit.* When one spouse passes away, the survivor is able to receive the larger of the two benefit amounts.
- *Restricted Application.* A higher-earning spouse may be able to start collecting a spousal benefit on the lower-earning spouse's benefit while allowing his or her benefit to continue to grow. Due to the Bipartisan Budget Act of 2015, this option is only available to individuals who turned age 62 before January 1, 2016.

In November of 2015, the Bipartisan Budget Act of 2015 was passed, which will have a dramatic impact on the way many Americans plan for Social Security. As the largest change to Social Security since 2000, the Bipartisan Budget Act of 2015 eliminated an estimated $9.5 billion* of benefits to retirees and may

---

* *http://www.nasdaq.com/article/congress-planning-to-close-social-security-loopholes-cm536252*

limit some of the flexibility you previously had to structure your benefits.

In 2000, Congress passed the Senior Citizens Freedom to Work Act. The bill allowed retirees to suspend receiving benefits so they wouldn't be subject to additional taxation if they chose to return to work after they filed for Social Security. However, by doing so, the bill also unintentionally created several loopholes in claiming strategies: most notably, the Restricted Application for spousal benefits and "file and suspend" filing strategy. For most Americans, the Bipartisan Budget Act of 2015 closed these loopholes by eliminating "file and suspend" and the Restricted Application.

The new rules mandate that:
- If a primary worker is not currently receiving benefits, then their dependents (child, spouse) can no longer collect benefits based on the primary worker's earning record.
- If you file for benefits, then you are filing for all benefits to which you are entitled – not just the benefit type you choose.

It's important to remember that in spite of these immense changes, one thing stayed the same – filing for Social Security is one of the most important financial decisions you will make in your lifetime, and a financial professional can help ensure you make the right one.

THE DIVORCE FACTOR

How does a divorced spouse qualify for benefits? If you have gone through a divorce, it might affect the retirement benefit to which you are entitled.

In general, a person can receive benefits as a divorced spouse on a former spouse's Social Security record so long as the following conditions are met:

- the marriage lasted at least 10 years; and
- the person filing for divorce benefits is at least age 62, unmarried, and not entitled to a higher Social Security benefit on his or her own record.*

With all of the different options, strategies and benefits to choose from, you can see why filing for Social Security is more complicated than just mailing in the paperwork. Gathering the data and making yourself aware of all your different options isn't enough to know exactly what to do, however. On the one hand, you can knock yourself out trying to figure out which options are best for you and wondering if you made the best decision.

On the other hand, you can work with a financial professional who uses customized software that takes all the variables of your specific situation into account and calculates your best option. You have tens of thousands of different options for filing for your Social Security benefit. If your spouse is a different age than you are, it nearly doubles the amount of options you have. This is far more complicated arithmetic than most people can do on their own.

If you want a truly accurate understanding of when and how to file, you need someone who will ask you the right questions about your situation, someone who has access to specialized software that can crunch the numbers. The reality is that you need to work with a professional that can provide you with the sophisticated analysis of your situation that will help you make a truly informed decision.

---

* *http://www.ssa.gov/retire2/yourdivspouse.htm*

Important Questions about Your Social Security Benefit:

- How can I maximize my lifetime benefit? By knowing when and how to file for Social Security. This usually means waiting until you have at least reached your Full Retirement Age. A professional has the experience and the tools to help determine when and how you can maximize your lifetime benefits.
- Who will provide reliable advice for making these decisions? Only a professional has the tools and experience to provide you reliable advice.
- Will the Social Security Administration provide me with the advice? The Social Security Administration cannot provide you with advice or strategies for claiming your benefit. They can give you information about your monthly benefit, but that's it. They also don't have the tools to tell you what your specific best option is. They can accurately answer how the system works, but they can't advise you on what decision to make as to how and when to file for benefits.

The Maximization Report that your financial professional will generate represents an invaluable resource for understanding how and when to file for your Social Security benefit. When you get your customized Social Security Maximization Report, you will not only know all the options available to you – but you will understand the financial implications of each choice. In addition to the analysis, you will also get a report that shows exactly at what age – including which month and year – you should trigger benefits and how you should apply. It also includes a variety of other time-specific recommendations, such as when to apply for Medicare or take Required Minimum Distributions from your qualified plans. A report means there is no need to wonder, or to try to figure out when to take action – the Social Security Maximization Report lays it all out for you in plain English.

CHAPTER 4 RECAP //

- To get the most out of your Social Security benefit, you need to file at the right time.
- A financial professional can help you determine when you should file for Social Security to get your Maximum Lifetime Benefit.

5

WILL SOCIAL SECURITY BE ENOUGH?
FILLING THE INCOME GAP

The moment that you stop working and start living off the money that you've set aside for retirement can be referred to as the Retirement Cliff. You've worked and earned money your whole life, but the day that you retire, that income comes to an end. That's the day that you have to have other assets that fill the gap. Social Security will fill in some, but you need to come up with something else. After you have calculated your Social Security benefit and have selected the year and month that will maximize your lifetime benefits, it's time to look at your other retirement assets, incomes and options that will reduce or eliminate the drop-off of the Retirement Cliff. You may have a pension, an IRA or Roth

IRA, dividends from stock holdings, money from the sale of real estate, rental property, or other sources of income. What other sources of reliable income do you have?

If your monthly Social Security check and your other supplemental income leave a shortfall in your *desired* income, how are you going to fix it? This shortfall is called the **Income Gap** and it needs to be filled in order to maintain your lifestyle into retirement. If you have a known income gap that you need to fill, you want to know how to fill that income gap with the fewest dollars possible. You basically want to buy that income gap for the least amount of money possible. You don't want it to cost you too much, because you want to get the most out of your other assets, including planning for your future and planning for your legacy. You do that by maximizing your Social Security benefit, leveraging your additional income and looking at other investment tools that can help generate income for you. Your specific needs, of course, should be analyzed and consulted by a professional.

TAKING A HYBRID APPROACH TO YOUR INCOME NEEDS

You looked at Social Security strategies earlier, discovering you have some control over how and when you file. Those decisions can change the outcome of your benefit in your favor. Once you start drawing that income, it is safer and will provide you with a reliable source of income for the rest of your life. While there are many factors of Social Security that you can control, there are many that you cannot.

For example, you do not have the choice of putting more money into Social Security in order to get more out of it. If you could have the option to contribute more money toward Social Security in order to secure a guaranteed income, it would be a great way to create a Green Money asset that would enhance your retirement. Since that option isn't available, you may seek an investment tool that is similar to Social Security that provides you with a reliable income. It also has the potential to increase the value of your principal investment! This kind of win-win situation exists, and it's called an annuity.

Today, you probably have savings in a variety of assets that you acquired over the years. But you may not have taken time to examine them and assess how they will support your retirement.

It's not about whether the market goes up or down, but when it does. If it goes down at the wrong time for your five or 10 year retirement horizon, you could be in serious danger of losing some of your retirement income.

If you have assets that you would like to structure for retirement income, *an annuity may be the right choice for you.*

Ask yourself the following questions:
- How concerned are you about finding a secure financial vehicle to protect your savings?
- If a spouse passes away soon or in the future, what income will be lost and what is the best way to replace it?
- If you live into your 90s, do you have a plan to guarantee you'll still have enough income?
- How concerned are you that there may be a better way to structure your savings?

If you are concerned about the best way to fill your income gap, an income annuity investment tool is likely a good option for you. Income annuities have many similar qualities to Social Security that give them the same look and feel as that reliable benefit check you get every month. Most importantly, an income annuity can be an efficient and profitable way to solve your income gap.

HOW ANNUITIES FIT INTO AN OVERALL INCOME PLAN

Annuities are popular and reliable investment tools that allow you to secure income during retirement. In its simplest form, an annuity is a way to invest your money that allows you to structure it for income. Annuities come in a variety of modes. Finding the right one for you will take a conversation with your financial professional. Be sure you fully understand the features, benefits and costs of any annuity you are considering before investing money.

Here is how they can work:

When you put your money into an annuity, you are essentially buying an investment product from an insurance company. It is a contract between you and the insurance company that provides the investment tool. Let's say you have saved $100,000 and need it to generate income to meet your needs above and beyond your Social Security and pension checks. You give the $100,000 to an insurance company, who in turn invests it to generate growth. They usually select investments that have modest returns over long term horizons. In other words, they generally put it somewhere stable and predictable. Most commonly, they will invest it in a combination of bonds and treasuries that are safer and dependable ways to grow money. They use the money from the insurance products they sell to invest, use a portion of the returns to generate profits for themselves, and return a portion to clients in the form of payouts, claims, and structured income options.

One of the most attractive qualities of these types of annuities is something called annual reset. Annual reset is sometimes also referred to as a "ratcheting." Instead of taking on the risk that comes with putting money in a fluctuating market, you can offset that risk onto the insurance company. It works like this: If the market goes down, you don't suffer a loss. Instead, the insurance company absorbs it. But if the market goes up, you share with the insurance company some of the profit made on the gain. The amount of gain you get is called your annuity participation rate. Typically the insurer will cap the amount of gain you can realize at somewhere between 3 and 7 percent. If the market goes up 10 percent, you would realize a portion of that gain (whatever percentage you are capped at). This means you never lose money on your investment, while always gaining a portion of the upswings. The measurement period of your annuity can be calculated monthly, weekly and even daily, but most annuities are measured annually. The level of the index when you buy and the index level one year later will determine the amount of loss or gain. You and the insurance company are betting that the market will generally go up over time.

INCOME RIDER

When you use that $100,000 to buy a contract with an insurance company in the form of an annuity, you are pegging your money on an index. It could be the S&P 500, the Dow Jones Industrial Average or any number of indexes. To generate income from the annuity, you select something called an income rider. An income rider is a subset of an indexed annuity. Essentially, it is the amount of money from which the insurance company will pay you an income while you have your money in their annuity. Your income rider is a larger number than what your investment is actually worth, and if you select the income rider, it will increase in value over time, providing you with more income. As the insurance company holds your money and invests it, they generate a return on it that they use to pay you a regular monthly income based on a higher number. The insurance company has to outperform the amount that they pay you in order to make a profit.

Remember, insurance companies make long-term investments that provide them with predictable flows of money. They like to stabilize the amount of money that goes in and out of their doors instead of paying and receiving large unpredictable chunks at once. When you opt for an income rider, an insurance company can reliably predict how much money they will pay out to you over a set period of time. It's predictable, and they like that. They can base their business on those predictable numbers.

In order to encourage investors to leave their money in their annuity contracts, insurance companies create surrender periods that protect their investments. If you remove your money from the annuity contract during the surrender period, you will pay a penalty and will not be able to receive your entire investment amount back. A typical surrender period is 10 years. If after three years you decide that you want your $100,000 back, the insurance company has that money tied up in bonds and other investments with the understanding that they will have it for another seven years. Because they will take a hit on removing the money from their investments prematurely, you will have to pay a surrender charge that makes up for their loss. During the surrender period, an annuity is not a demand deposit account like a savings or checking account. The higher returns that you are guaranteed from an annuity are dependent on the timeframe you selected. The longer an insurance company can hold your money, the easier it is for them to guarantee a predictable return on it.

If you leave your money in the annuity contract, you get a reliable monthly income no matter what happens in the market. Once the surrender period has expired, you can remove your money whenever you want. Your money becomes liquid again because the insurance company has used it in an investment that fit the timeline of your surrender period. For many people, this is an attractive trade-off that can provide a creative solution for filling their income gap.

When is an annuity with an income rider right for you? A good financial professional can help you make that determination by taking the time to listen closely to your situation and understanding what your needs are as you enter retirement. Every salesperson has a bag full of brochures and PowerPoint presentations, but they need to know exactly what the financial concerns of their individual clients are in order to help them make the most informed and beneficial decision. Some people need income today, others need it in five or 10 years. Others may have their income needs met but are planning to move closer to their children and will need to buy a house in 10 years. Or, if you want income in 15 years, you might want to choose a different investment product for 10 years, and then switch to an annuity with an income rider during the last five years of your timeline. Everyone's situation is different and everyone's needs are different. People who are interested in annuities, however, usually need to make decisions that affect their income needs, whether it is filling their income gap, or providing for income down the road.

In Chapter 1 when you read about organizing your assets, your attention was brought to how much risk your portfolio was exposed to. Organizing your assets to reflect your needs, especially for income, is one of the most important steps in creating a retirement plan. If you are in or near retirement, it is likely that many of your investment products are focused on income generation. If you are on a fixed income, you need to create a plan to increase your income to keep pace with the cost of living, including inflation and the rising price of goods and services.

Annuities can be an important tool for making the transition to retirement. Income is something that has to be predictable and guaranteed. The right annuity can provide you with income that will last as long as you live. By contrast, depending on the stock market for income can deplete the value of your investment, especially if the market takes a turn for the worse.

What happens if you place a shorter timeframe on those assets from which you need to draw an income? Something called single premium immediate annuities may be for you:

SINGLE PREMIUM IMMEDIATE ANNUITIES (SPIA)

A single premium immediate annuity is simply a contract between you and an insurance company. SPIAs are structured so that you pay a lump sum of money (a single premium) to an insurance company, and they give you a guaranteed income over an agreed upon time period. That time period could be five years, or it could be for the remainder of your lifetime. Guarantees from insurance companies are based on the claims-paying ability of the issuing insurance company.

SPIAs provide investors with a stream of reliable income when they can't afford to take the risk of losing money in a fluctuating market. While there is general faith that the market always trends up, at least in the long-term, if you are focusing on income over a shorter period of time, you may not be able to take a big hit in the market. Beyond normal market volatility, interest rates also come with an inherent level of uncertainty, making it hard to create a dependable income on your own. SPIAs reduce risk for you by giving you regular monthly, quarterly or yearly payments that can begin the moment you buy the contract. Your financial professional can walk you through a series of different payment options to help you select the one that most closely fits your needs.

WHAT ARE FIXED INDEXED ANNUITIES?

A new class of annuity is offered by insurance companies that provides a portion of the stock index performance along with a no-loss provision. This product is called the fixed indexed annuity. This is not a security, but a single-premium traditional annuity, and is classified as such because of the strict insurance department requirements it meets for interest guarantees and guarantees against loss of principal. It also provides traditional annuity benefits like tax-deferred growth, yearly withdrawal of funds without penalty, and no management or administrative fees.

Fixed indexed annuities also offer:

- A no loss provision, meaning that premium payments and credited interest never lose value.
- Participation rates that vary from no cap to a fixed percentage. Participation rates are the percentage of earnings your annuity shares in from the insurance company's stock market investments. You participate in the upswings, but are not exposed to any loss experienced by the insurer. This allows you to benefit from higher returns with a guarantee of no loss of value.
- Rates of return that are competitive. Many investment accounts struggle to keep up with inflation. A fixed indexed annuity can often provide higher returns while guaranteeing the value of your premium and the interest it gains.

WHY THE RIGHT ANNUITIES ARE GOOD INVESTMENTS FOR SENIORS

There are plenty of articles outlining why seniors should not own annuities. Those articles don't tell the whole story, however. Some annuities are excellent investments for seniors. They do not charge high annual fees, will not lose money and they grow every year even in down markets. Some even guarantee a set rate for a specified time, just like a bank CD or IRA. This type of annuity can be an excellent investment for seniors looking for higher interest rates than banks offer.

They offer tax deferral, more liquidity than a CD, avoid probate when a beneficiary is properly designated, compound interest, and can never lose the annual gains. There are no surrender charges upon death, either. The right annuity can be a great way to transfer more wealth to heirs, but just like there are bad stocks, bonds, and mutual funds, there are bad annuities. That doesn't mean there aren't good ones, however. One mistake that many seniors make when investing in annuities is trusting the name of the insurance company or bank instead of the annuity itself. While you should work with a financially strong company, you also need a good annuity. An independent consultant or advisor with integrity can screen them for you and recommend the best one for your situation.

- An annuity portfolio provides seniors with a special peace of mind. It provides substantial guaranteed growth without generating annual 1099s, thereby <u>reducing</u> annual taxes! Each year the growth of annuities is credited and locked in. Additionally, annuities are protected by the guarantee fund of your state.

- Unlike variable annuities, a better type of annuity bears no administrative fees, no annual maintenance fees, no upkeep expenses, no buy or sell expenses, and no management fees.

- An annuity is protected for you, your spouse, children and grandchildren from bankruptcy, creditor's claims and lawsuits that may arise in your estate when you are no longer there to defend it.

- Unlike the stock market, you do not have to worry about which way the market is moving. You do not have to know when to cash out for a gain, nor do you have to know when to sell and cut losses. You have a no-loss guarantee. Your principal is protected.

- Insurance companies have the legally required reserves and the financial strength to provide the guarantees of their annuity products, in addition to paying into the various state guarantee funds.

Additional Annuity Information:
- Some contracts will allow you to draw income from the term high point or high water mark that the market reaches

COMPARISON OF FIXED ANNUITIES WITH CERTIFICATES OF DEPOSIT (CDS)

FEATURES	INDEX OR FIXED ANNUITIES (NOT VARIABLE)	CDS / SAVINGS / MONEY MARKET
Free from principal/market risk and price fluctuations?	Y	Y
Are interest earnings free from current taxation?	Y	N
Are interest earnings reinvested automatically with no current income taxation?	Y	N
Am I able to make small additional investments?	Y In Some Cases	N In Most Cases
Is tax liability on Social Security income eliminated on deferred annuities?	Y	N
Are the assets liquid?	Y A Surrender Charge May Apply	Y
Are they flexible?	Y	Y
Is there penalty-free withdrawal?	Y	N
Are funds reduced by commissions?	N	N
Does this investment automatically avoid the expense and delay of probate?	Y When Beneficiaries are Properly Designated	N
Is there guaranteed lifetime income with tax advantages?	Y	N

71

each year. The income rider will then begin calculating its value from the high water mark.

- Variable annuities, however, can lose money with market fluctuations. As their name suggests, they vary with the market. These annuities do not take advantage of annual reset when the market goes down. The income rider will stay the same, but the value of your actual contract may fall. If you surrender the annuity, the insurance company will pay you the market value of the asset, regardless of whether it matches, exceeds or falls short of the value at which you bought the contract. If its value has dropped significantly, you may be better off taking the income rider without surrendering your contract.

- Income annuities are investment tools that look and feel a bit like Social Security. Every year you allow the money to grow with the market, it will "roll up" by a specific amount, paying out a specific percent to you as income each year.

- Annuities can work very well to create income, and a financial professional can help you find the one that best matches your income need, and can also structure it to work for you.

CLEARING UP MISUNDERSTANDINGS ABOUT ANNUITIES

Have you seen ads like these: Never Die Owning an Annuity, What the IRS Doesn't Want You to Know About Annuities, or Annuity Owner Mistakes? The purpose of these publications is to scare investors into thinking that all annuities are bad investment decisions. The following are untruths about annuities:

- Uncle Sam will tax all of your annuity money when you die.
- Annuities include life insurance.

- All annuities are long term.
- Annuities are only for younger people.
- All annuities are unsafe and risky.
- Insurance companies keep your money in your annuity when you die.
- You are unable to access your money.
- You have to take out payments on all annuities and you can never take it out in a lump sum.

As you can tell from the list above, there are many misconceptions and untruths about annuities. Here are the facts:

Many annuities are:

- Tax deferred ways to grow wealth, which can help reduce your annual taxes.
- Insured by State Guarantee Funds and other layers of safety (ask your agent or advisor for details).
- Variable annuities are not insured.
- Funds that avoid probate upon death.
- Investment products that have cash withdrawal privileges without penalty (including monthly, quarterly, semi-annually, and annually).
- Available with guaranteed rates, and guaranteed monthly income.
- Available in a lump sum upon maturity.
- Able to provide a bonus rate upon deposit and in some cases future deposits for up to five or six years.

When used properly, the right annuity can provide you with more benefits and features than are offered by CDs, bonds, or mutual funds. Seek an independent annuity expert to receive the pros and cons of all types of annuities.

Managing Risk Within Your Annuity:

Just like any investment strategy, the amount of risk needs to fit the comfort level of the investor. Annuities are no exception. Without going into too much detail, here are some additional ways to manage risk with annuity options:

- If you want to structure an annuity investment for growth over a long period of time, you can select a variable annuity. The value of your principal investment follows the market and can lose or gain value with the market. This type of annuity can also have an income rider, but it is really more useful as an accumulation tool that bets on an improving market. A 40-year-old couple, for example, will probably want to structure more for growth and take on more risk than someone in their 70s. The 40-year-old couple may select a variable annuity with an income rider that kicks in when they plan to retire. If it rises with the market or outperforms it, the value of their investment has grown. If the market loses ground over the duration of the contract or their annuity underperforms, they can still rely on the income rider. Variable annuities can have very high fees. Make sure you get the facts and don't invest just because the product is sold by a large, well known company.

- If you are 60 years old and you have more immediate income needs that you need to come up with above and beyond your Social Security, you need a low risk, reliable source of income. If you choose an annuity option, you are looking for something that will pay out an income right away over a relatively short timeframe. You probably want to opt for an SPIA, an indexed annuity with an income rider, or a split annuity that pays you immediately and spans a five-year period, as well as an additional annuity that begins paying you in five years, and another longer term annuity that begins paying you in 10 years. Bear in mind that each annuity contract has its own costs and fees. Review these with your financial professional before you determine the best products and strategies for your situation.

The following example shows just how helpful an indexed annuity option can be for a retiree:

> » *Bob and Mary are 62 years old and have decided to run the numbers to see what their retirement is going to look like. They know they currently need $6,000 per month to pay their bills and maintain their current lifestyle. They have also done their Social Security homework and have determined that, between the two of them, they will receive $4,200 per month in benefits. They also receive $350 per month in rent from a tenant who lives in a small carriage house in their backyard. Between their Social Security and the monthly rent income, they will be short $1,450 per month.*
>
> *They do have an additional asset, however. They have been contributing for years to an IRA that has reached a value of $350,000. They realize that they have to figure out how to turn the $350,000 in their IRA into $1,450 per month for the rest of their life. At first glance, it may seem like they will have plenty of money. With some quick calculations, they find they have 240 months, or nearly 20 years, of monthly income before they exhaust the account. When you consider income tax, the potential for higher taxes in the future, and market fluctuations (because many IRAs are invested in the market), the amount in the IRA seems to have a little less clout. Every dollar Bob and Mary take out of the IRA is subject to income tax, and if they leave the remainder in the IRA, they run the risk of losing money in a volatile market. Once they retire and*

*stop getting a paycheck every two weeks, they also stop con-
tributing to their IRA. And when they aren't supplementing
its growth with their own money, they are entirely dependent
on market growth. That's a scary prospect. They could also
withdraw the money from the IRA and put it in a savings
account or CD, but removing all the money at once will put
them in a tax bracket that will claim a huge portion of the
value of the IRA. A seemingly straightforward asset has now
become a complicated equation. Bob and Mary didn't know
what to do, so they met with their financial professional.*

*Their financial professional suggested that they use the
money to purchase an indexed annuity with an income rider.
They selected an annuity that was designed for their specific
situation. They took the lump sum from their IRA, placed it
in an indexed annuity taking advantage of annual reset so
they never lost the value of their investment. In return, they
were guaranteed the $1,450 of income per month that they
needed to meet their retirement goals. The simplicity of the
contract allowed them to do an analysis with their professional just once to understand the product. They basically put
their money in an investment crockpot where they didn't have
to look at it or manage it. They just needed to let it simmer.
In fact, their professional was able to find an annuity for
them that allowed them their $1,450 monthly payment with
a lump sum of $249,455, leaving them more than $100,000
to reinvest somewhere else. Keep in mind that annuities are
tax deferred, meaning you will pay tax on the income you
receive from an annuity in the year you receive it.*

*» Tanya is 60 years old and is wondering how she can use
her assets to provide her with a retirement income. She has a
$5,000 per month income need. If she starts withdrawing her
Social Security benefit in six years at age 66, it will provide*

her with $2,200 per month. She also has a pension that kicks in at age 70 that will give her another $1,320 per month. That leaves an income gap of $2,800 from ages 66 to 69, and then an income gap of $1,480 at age 70 and beyond. If Tanya uses only Green Money to solve her income need, she will need to deposit $918,360 at 2 percent interest to meet her monthly goal for her lifetime. If she opts to use Red Money and withdraws the amount she needs each month from the market, let's say the S & P 500, she will run out of cash in 10 years if she invested between the years of 2000 and 2012. Suffering a market downturn like that during the period for which she is relying on it for retirement income will change her life, and not for the better.

Working with a financial professional to find a better way, Tanya found that she could take a hybrid approach to fill her income gap. Her professional recommended two different income vehicles: one that allowed her to deposit just $190,161 with a 2 percent return, and one that was a $146,000 income annuity. These tools filled her income gap with $336,161, requiring her to spend $582,000 less money to accomplish her goal! Working with a professional to find the right tools for her retirement needs saved Tanya over half a million dollars.

CREATING AN INCOME PLAN

Creating an income plan before you retire allows you to satisfy your need for lifetime income and ensures that your lifestyle can last as long as you do. You also want to create a plan that operates in the most efficient way possible. Doing so will give more security to your Need Later Money and will potentially allow you to build your legacy down the road. Rolling over a portion of your 401(k) or 403(b) while working (it is called an in-service rollover) is a great way to plan ahead for more retirement income and not lose this money that would have remained in your retirement account with your employer.

WHAT YOU SHOULD DO BEFORE AND AFTER THE DEATH OF A SPOUSE

When faced with the loss of a spouse, simple things can suddenly seem complex and overwhelming. A death can leave a person alone without family nearby. It also creates a situation that requires immediate adjustment.

Some couples plan ahead for this day, making the transition seamless and less stressful. Many couples procrastinate, thinking they have time or that an untimely passing won't happen to one of them. One will be financially comfortable, while the other may struggle because they weren't involved in crafting the plan for the finances and a plan to replace lost income was not in place.

Knowing what to do with various inherited funds requires guidance. Avoiding penalties, minimizing taxation, and redefining the level of risk for what is left will have a positive effect on their hard-earned nest egg. Expenses will change and the life expectancy of the surviving spouse may be long. The two major fears that concern all retirees are outliving their money and losing their money to costly nursing homes.

Creating a plan now will be comforting when a spouse unexpectedly passes away. A sense of relief is felt twice: when the plan that has been postponed is finally completed, and also when the widowed spouse has the peace of mind of knowing that their future is secure.

Here are some steps that will help you or your spouse financially cope:

- **Make an inventory of your physical and non-physical items.** Inventory the items of value in your home in the form of a list. Things like computers, jewelry, electronics, guns, and collectibles should all be listed. Non-physical items, including 401(k)s, brokerage accounts, IRA assets, life insurance policies, annuities, etc., should also be included in a comprehensive list.

- **Understand your Social Security situation.** Gather information about your spouses' employer, the approximate earnings over the previous two years, where tax returns are kept, and where marriage certificates and Social Security cards are located. Additionally, lump sum benefits and/or monthly benefit payments could be possible for spouses and children.

- **Keep your important papers safe.** Your stock and bond certificates, power of attorney documents, partnership papers, trust, wills, bank documents, insurance policies, medical records, health care advance directives and other papers should all be organized and easy to locate when you need them.

- **Update your beneficiaries.** Ensuring that your assets are transferred according to your wishes may require more than a will. Beneficiary designations on assets are necessary to ensure that your life insurance policies, 401(k)s, annuities and other types of assets go where you intend them to.

- **Have the important conversations.** Let your wishes be known to your family and loved ones. Discussing the organization of your assets and your estate will help ensure that your legacy is passed on the way you intend it to be.

- **Consolidate.** Your financial records, including financial institutions and account numbers, Social Security cards/numbers, passwords to online accounts, and answers to security questions should be consolidated in one place.

- **Work with a retirement planning expert you trust.** Developing a plan that will smoothly transition your assets to your beneficiaries in ways that preserve their value starts with working with a financial professional you can trust.

Here is a basic roadmap of what we have covered so far:

- Review your income needs and look specifically at the shortfall you may have during each year of your retirement based on your Social Security income, and income from any other assets you have. Create an income plan that will replace lost income when a spouse dies and one that will provide income into your 90s.
- Ask yourself where you are in your distribution phase. Is retirement one year away? 10 years away? Last year?
- Determine how much money you need and how you need to structure your existing assets to provide for that need in a tax-efficient manner.
- If you have an asset from which you need to generate income, consider options offered by purchasing an income rider on an annuity.
- Be sure <u>not</u> to take income from growth accounts. When there's a correction, the losses plus your withdrawals will cause your portfolio to deplete much faster. Better to set up a separate account just for income.

CHAPTER 5 RECAP //

- Having an income plan will help you get a picture of what your retirement is really going to look like.
- You have *Need Now Money* needs and *Need Later Money* needs. Creating an income plan is the first step toward providing for both of these needs.
- Maximizing your Social Security benefit depends on *when* and *how* you file.
- You'll need to examine your specific situation to find the best option for you.
- It's not impossible for you to calculate when the opportune time would be to trigger your Social Security income. In fact, with the tools and advice of a financial professional, it's quite easy.
- Integrating your Social Security options with the rest of your income plan will give you an idea of how much more money you need.
- Every dollar your Social Security income increases is less money you'll have to spend from your nest egg to supplement your income.
- After Social Security and your additional income are accounted for, the amount that's left to meet your needs is called the *Income Gap*.
- It is important to find ways to leverage your retirement assets to satisfy your need for lifetime income.
- It has been ages since many stocks returned meaningful dividends, so it isn't advisable to rely on them for income. However, without some stocks in your portfolio, your retirement plan will likely lose ground to inflation.
- It might be very attractive to have another asset, such as an annuity, that is designed to give you a reliable and guaranteed income. That income can go up in value as you wait to trigger a monthly check.

- If you think maximizing your Social Security isn't enough and you need the rest of your assets to be optimized to fill the income gap, an annuity may be a good option for you.
- Creating a retirement plan that focuses only on providing income will eventually have you cutting into your principal, drying it up over time and leaving you with very little money.
- Although an annuity is an income-producing asset that does not subject your income to market risk, it still has the opportunity to grow.
- Be sure you understand the features, benefits, costs and fees associated with any annuity or other investment product before you invest.
- Consider doing an in-service rollover with a portion of your employer's retirement plan to create more income for when you retire and to protect that money from stock market losses as you approach retirement.
- Plan now (well in advance) for replacing lost income when your spouse passes away and to assure you will receive a check until you die. All unused money will go to your heirs (unlike taking payments from your employers retirement or pension plan, your children cannot inherit the money).

6

ACCUMULATION

Understanding your Social Security benefit, filling the income gap and making an overall plan that meets your retirement income needs is no small task. Once you have worked with a financial professional to structure your income needs, it's time to take a look at the future. With your immediate income needs met, you have the opportunity to take your additional assets and leverage them for profit to supplement your income in the future, to prepare for anticipated health care costs or to contribute to your legacy. Stable income also means that you should have the staying power to stick with your investment portfolio through the ups and downs in the market.

MATH OF REBOUNDS (RECOVERING LOSSES)

A fickle market can raise the eyebrows of even the most veteran investor. Taking a hit in the market hurts no matter how stable your income. Part of the pain comes from knowing that when you take a step back in the market, it requires an even larger step forward to return to where you were. As the market goes up and down, those larger gains you need to realize to get back to zero start to look even more daunting.

HOW REAL PEOPLE MAKE INVESTMENT DECISIONS

It can be challenging to watch the stock market's erratic changes every month, week or even every day. When you have your money riding on it, the ride can feel pretty bumpy. When you are managing your money by yourself, emotions inevitably enter into the mix. The Dow Jones Industrial Average and the S&P 500 represent more to you than market fluctuations. They represent a portion of your retirement. It's hard not to be emotional about it.

Everyone knows you should buy low and sell high. But this is what is more likely to happen:

The market takes a downturn, similar to the 2008 crash, and investors see as much as a 30 percent loss in their stock holdings. It's hard to watch, and it's harder to bear the pain of losing that much money. The math of rebounds means that they will need to rely on even larger gains just to get back to where things were before the downturn. They sell. But eventually, and inevitably, the market begins to rise again. Maybe slowly, maybe with some moderate growth, but by the time the average investor notices an upward trend and wants to buy in again, they have already missed many gains.

CHAPTER 6 RECAP //

- After your retirement income need is met, you can plan to accumulate wealth from your remaining assets.
- Managing money by yourself can lead to emotional investing, which can create unreliable results.

7

WHAT IS YELLOW MONEY?

Now that you've calculated the Rule of 100, determined how much risk you have and how much you want, and you've determined how much Green Money you need to meet your short-term and mid-term income needs, it's time to look at what you have left. The money you have left after you've calculated your Green Money needs has the potential of becoming Red Money: your stocks, mutual funds and other investment products that you want to continue using to accumulate value with the market. You now have the luxury of taking a closer second look at your Red Money to determine how you would like to manage it.

The deck is stacked against the individual investor. The average investor on a fixed income failed to keep pace with inflation in nine of the last 14 years, meaning the inherent risk in managing your Red Money is very real and could have a lasting impact on your assets.

So, how much of your Red Money do you invest, and in what kinds of markets, investment products and stocks do you invest? There are a lot of different directions in which you can take your Red Money. One thing is certain: significant accumulation depends on investing in the market. How you go about doing it is different for everyone. Gathering stocks, bonds and investment funds together in a portfolio without a cohesive strategy behind them could cause you to miss out on the benefits of a more thoughtful and planned approach. The end result is that you may never really understand what your money is doing, where and how it is really invested, and which investment principles are behind the investment products you hold. While you may have goals for each individual piece of your portfolio, it is likely that you don't have a comprehensive plan for your Red Money, which may mean that *you are taking on more risk than you would like, and are getting less return for it than is possible.*

Enter **Yellow Money.** Yellow Money is money that is managed by a professional *with a purpose.* After your income needs are met and you have assets that you would like to dedicate to accumulation, there are decisions you need to make about how to invest those assets. You can invest in stocks, index funds, mutual funds, bonds—you name it. However, the difference between Red Money and Yellow Money is that Yellow Money has a cohesive strategy behind it that is *implemented by a professional.* When you manage your Red Money with an investment plan, it becomes Yellow Money: *money that is being managed with a specific purpose, a specific set of focused goals and a specific strategy in mind.* Yellow Money is still a type of Red Money. It comes with different levels of risk. But Yellow Money is under the watchful eye of professionals who have a stake in the success of your money in the market and who can recommend a range of strategies from those designed for preservation to those targeting rapid growth. You don't want to miss out on achieving the right level of risk, and more importantly, composing a careful plan for the return of your assets.

It can be helpful to think of Red Money and Yellow Money with this analogy:

If you need to travel through an unfamiliar city in a foreign country, you could rent a car or perhaps hire a driver. Were you to drive yourself, you would try to gain guidance from perplexing road signs and need to adhere to traffic rules—with no experience or assistance to lean on. It would take longer to get to where you want to go, and the chance of a traffic accident would be higher. If you hired a driver, they would manage your journey. A driver would know the route, how to avoid traffic, and follow the rules of the road.

Red Money is like driving yourself. With Yellow Money, you are still traveling by car, but now you have a professional working on your behalf.

TAKING A CLOSER LOOK AT YOUR PORTFOLIO

Think about your investment portfolio. Think specifically of what you would consider your Red Money. Do you know what is there? You may have several different investment products like individual mutual funds, bond accounts, stocks, etc. You may have inherited a stock portfolio from a relative, or you might be invested in a bond account offered by the company for which you worked due to your familiarity with them. While you may or may not be managing your investments individually, the reality is that you probably don't have an overall management strategy for all of your investments. Investments that aren't managed are simply Red Money, or money that is at risk in the market. Harnessing the earning potential of your Red Money relies on more than a collection of stocks and bonds, however. It needs guided management.

A good Yellow Money manager uses the knowledge they have about the level of risk with which you are comfortable, what you need or want to use your money for, when you want it or need it and how you want to use it. The Yellow Money options that they choose for you will still have a certain level of risk, but under the right management, control and process, you have a far better chance of a successful outcome that meets your specific needs.

When you meet with an investment professional, you can look at all of your assets together. Chances are that you have accumulated a number of different assets over the last several years. You may have a 401(k), an IRA, a Roth IRA, an account of self-directed stocks, a brokerage account, etc. Wherever you put your money, a financial professional will review your assets and help you determine the level of risk to which you are exposed now and should be exposed to in the future.

Here is a typical example of how an investment professional can be helpful to a future retiree with Yellow Money needs:

> » *Janet is 65 years old and wants to retire in two years. She has a 401(k) from her job to which she has contributed for 26 years. She also has some stocks that her late husband managed. Janet also has $55,000 in a mutual fund that her sister recommended to her five years ago and $30,000 in another mutual fund that she heard about at work. She takes a look at her assets one day and decides that she doesn't understand what they add up to or what kind of retirement they will provide. She decides to meet with an investment professional. Janet's professional immediately asks her:*
>
> **1. Do you know exactly where all of your money is?** *Janet doesn't know much about all her husband's stocks, which have now become hers. Their value is at $100,000 invested in three large cap companies. Janet is unsure of the companies and whether she should hold or sell them.*

2. Do you know what types of assets you own? *Yes and no. She knows she had a 401(k) and IRAs, but she is unfamiliar with her husband's self-directed stock portfolio or the type of mutual funds she owns. Furthermore she is unclear as to how to manage the holdings as she nears retirement.*

3. Do you know the investment strategies behind each one of the products you own? *While Janet knows she had a 401(k), an IRA and mutual fund holdings, she doesn't know how her 401(k) is organized or how to make it more conservative as she nears retirement. She is unsure whether her IRA is a Roth or traditional variety and how to draw income from it. She really does not have specific investment principles guiding her investment decisions, and she doesn't know anything about her husband's individual stocks. One major concern for Janet is whether her family would be okay if she were not around.*

After determining Janet's assets, her financial professional prepares a consolidated report that lays out all of her assets for her to review and explains each one of them to her. Janet discovers that although she is two years away from retiring, her 401(k) is organized with an amount of risk with which she is not comfortable. Sixty percent of her 401(k) is at risk, far off the mark if we abide by the Rule of 100. Janet opts to be more conservative than the Rule of 100 suggests, as she will rely on her 401(k) for most of her immediate income needs after retirement. Janet's professional also points out several instances of overlap between her mutual funds. Janet learns that while she is comfortable with one of her mutual funds, she does not agree with the management principles of the other. In the end, Janet's professional helps her re-organize her 401(k) to secure more Green Money for her retirement income. Her professional also uses her mutual fund and her husband's stock assets to create a growth-oriented investment plan that Janet will rely on for Need Later Money in 15 years when she plans to relocate closer to her children and grandchildren. By creating an overall investment strategy, Janet is able to meet her targeted goals in retirement. Janet's financial professional works closely with her and her tax professional to minimize the tax impact of any asset sales.

Like Janet, you may have several savings vehicles: a 401(k), an IRA to which you regularly contribute, some mutual funds to which you make monthly contributions, etc. What is your overall investment strategy? Do you have one in place? Do you want one that will help you meet your retirement goals? Yellow Money looks at ALL your accounts and all their different strategies to create a plan that helps them work together. Your current investment situation may not reflect your wishes. As a matter of fact, it likely doesn't.

You may have a better understanding of your assets than Janet did, but even someone with an investment strategy can benefit from having a financial professional review their portfolio:

» *Charles is 69 years old. He retired four years ago. He relied on income from an IRA for three years in order to increase his Social Security benefit. He also made significant investments in 36 different mutual funds. He chose to diversify among the funds by selecting a portion for growth, another for good dividends, another that focused on promising small cap companies and a final portion that works like index funds. All the money that Charles had in mutual funds he considered Need Later Money that he wanted to rely on in his 80s. After the stock market took a hit in 2008, Charles lost some confidence in his investments and decided to sit down with a financial professional to see if his portfolio was able to recover.*

The professional Charles met with was able to determine what goals he had in mind. Specifically, the financial professional determined what Charles actually wanted and needed the money for, and when he needed it. His professional also looked inside each of the mutual funds and discovered several instances of overlap. While Charles had created diversity in his portfolio by selecting funds focused on different goals, he didn't account for overlap in the companies in which the funds were invested. Out of the 36 funds, his professional found that 20 owned nearly identical stock. While most of the companies were good investments, the high instance of overlap did not contribute to the healthy investment diversity that Charles wanted. Charles's financial professional also provided him with a report that explained the concentration ratio of his holdings (noting how much of his portfolio was contained within the top 25 stock holdings), the percentage of his portfolio that each company in which he invested represented (showing the percentage of net assets that each company made up as an overall position in his portfolio) and the portfolio date of his account (showing when the funds in his portfolio were last updated: as funds are required to report updates only twice per year, it was possible that some of his fund reports could be six months old).

Charles's professional consolidated his assets into one investment management strategy. This allowed Charles's investments to be managed by someone he trusted who knew his specific investment goals and needs. Eliminating redundancy and overlap in his portfolio was easy to do but difficult to detect since Charles had multiple funds with multiple brokerage firms. Charles sat down with a professional to see if his mutual funds could perform well, and he left with a consolidated management plan and a money manager that understood him personally. That's Yellow Money at its best.

AVOIDING EMOTIONAL INVESTING

There's no way around it; people get emotional about their money. And for good reason. You've spent your life working for it, exchanging your time and talent for it, and making decisions about how to invest it, save it and make it grow. The maintenance of your lifestyle and your plans for retirement all depend on it. The best investment strategies, however, don't rely on emotions. One of Yellow Money's greatest strengths lies in the fact that it is managed by someone who understands your needs and desires, but doesn't make decisions about your money under the influence of emotion.

A well-managed investment account meets your goals as a whole, not in individualized and piecemeal ways. Professional money managers do this by creating requirements for each type of investment in which they put your money. We'll call them "screens." Your money manager will run your holdings through the screens they have created to evaluate different types of investment strategies. A professionally managed account will only have holdings that meet the requirements laid out in the overall management plan that was designed to meet your investment goals. The holdings that don't make it through the screens, the ones that don't contribute to your investment goals, are sold and redistributed to investments that your financial professional has determined to be appropriate.

Different screens apply to different Yellow Money strategies. For example, if one of your goals is significant growth, which would require taking on more risk alongside the potential for more return, an investment professional would screen for companies that have high rates of revenue and sales growth, high earnings growth, rising profit margins, and innovative products. On the other hand, if you want your portfolio to be used for income, which would call for lower risk and less return, your professional would screen for dividend yield and sector diversification. Every investor has a different goal, and every goal requires a customized strategy that uses quantitative screens. A professional will create a portfolio that reflects your investment desires. If some of the current assets you own complement the strategies that your professional recommends, those will likely stay in your portfolio.

Screening your assets removes emotions from the equation. It removes attachment to underperforming or overly risky investments. Financial professionals aren't married to particular stocks or mutual funds for any reason. They go by the numbers and see your portfolio through a lens shaped by your retirement goals. Your professional understands your wants and needs, and creates an investment strategy that takes your life events and future plans into account. It's an excellent approach since it allows you to tap into the tools and resources of a professional who has built a career around successful investing. Managing money is a full time job and is best left to a professional money manager.

Removing emotions from investing also allows you to be unaffected by the day-to-day volatility of the market. Your financial professional doesn't ask where the market is going to be in a year, three years or a month from now. If you look at the value of the stock market from the beginning of the twentieth century to today, it's going up. Despite the Great Depression, despite the 1987 crash, despite the 2008 market downturn, the market, as a whole, trends up. Remember the major market downturn in 2008 when the market lost 30 percent of its value? Not only did it completely recover, it has far exceeded its 2008 value. Emotional investing led countless people to sell low as the market went down, and buy the same shares back when the market started to recover. That's an expensive way to do business. While you can't afford to lose money that you need in two, three or five years, your Need Later Money has time to grow. The best way to do so is to make it Yellow.

CREATING AN INVESTMENT STRATEGY

Just like Janet and Charles, chances are that you can benefit from taking a more managed investment approach tailored to your goals. Yellow Money is generally Need Later Money that you want to grow for needs you'll have in at least 10 years. You can work with your financial planner to create investments that meet your needs within different timeframes. You may need to rely on some of your Yellow Money in 10, 15 or 20 years, whether for additional income, a large purchase you plan on making or a vacation. Whatever you want it for, you will need it down the road. A financial professional can help you rescale the risk of your assets as they grow, helping you lock in your profits and secure a source of income you can depend on later.

So what does a Yellow Money account look like? Here's what it doesn't look like: a portfolio with 49 small cap mutual funds, a dozen individual stocks and an assortment of bond accounts. A brokerage account with a hodgepodge of investments, even if goal-oriented, is not a professionally managed account. It's still Red Money. Remember, Yellow Money is a professionally-managed account that has an overarching investment philosophy. When you look at making investments that will perform to meet your future income needs, the burning question becomes: How much should you have in the market and how should it be invested? Working with a professional will help you determine how much risk you should take, how to balance your assets so they will meet your goals and how to plan for the big ticket items, like health care expenses, that may be in your future. Yes, Yellow Money is exposed to risk, but by working with a professional, you can manage that risk in a productive way.

WHY YELLOW MONEY?

If you have met your immediate income needs for retirement, why bother with professionally managing your other assets? The money you have accumulated above and beyond your income needs probably has a greater purpose. It may be for your children or grandchildren. You may want to give money to a charity or organization that you admire. In short, you may want to craft your legacy. It would be advantageous to grow your assets in the best manner possible. A financial professional has built a career around managing money in profitable ways. They are experts under the supervision of the organization that they represent.

Turning to Yellow Money also means that you don't have to burden yourself with the time commitment, the stress, and the cost of determining how to manage your money. Yellow Money can help you better enjoy your retirement. Do you want to sit down in your home office every day and determine how to best allocate your assets, or do you want to be living your life while someone else manages your money for you? When the majority of your Red Money is managed with a specific purpose by a financial professional, you don't have to be worrying about which stocks to buy and sell today or tomorrow.

SEEKING FINANCIAL ADVICE: STOCK BROKERS VS. INVESTMENT ADVISOR REPRESENTATIVES

Investors basically have access to two types of advice in today's financial world: advice from stock brokers and advice given by investment advisors. Most investors, however, don't know the difference between types of advice and the people from whom they receive advice. Today, there are two primary types of advice offered to investors: advice given by a commission-based registered representative (brokers) and advice given by fee-based Investment Advisor Representatives. Unfortunately, many investors are not aware that a difference exists; nor have they been explained the distinction between the two types of advice. In a 2011 survey taken by TD Ameritrade, the top reasons investors choose to work with an independent registered investment advisor are:

- Registered Investment Advisors are required, as fiduciaries, to offer advice that is in the best interest of clients
- More personalized service and competitive fee structure offered at a Registered Investment Advisor firm
- Dissatisfaction with full commission brokers

The truth is that there is a great deal of difference between stock brokers and investment advisor representatives. For starters, investment advisor representatives are obligated to act in an investor's best interests in all aspects of a financial relationship. Confusion continues to exist among investors struggling to find the best financial advice out there and the most credible sources of advice. Here is some information to help clear up the confusion so you can find good advice from a professional you can trust:

- Investment advisor representatives have the fiduciary duty to act in a client's best interest at all times with every investment decision they make. Stock brokers and brokerage firms usually do not act as fiduciaries to their investors and are not obligated to make decisions that are entirely in the best interest of their customers. For example, if you decide you want to invest in precious metals, a stock broker would offer you a precious metals account from their firm. An Investment Advisor would find you a precious metals account that is the best fit for you based on the investment strategy of your portfolio.
- Investment advisors give their clients a Form ADV describing the methods that the professional uses to do business. An Investment Advisor also obtains client consent regarding any conflicts of interest that could exist with the business of the professional.
- Stock brokers and brokerage firms are not obligated to provide comparable types of disclosure to their customers.

- Whereas stock brokers and firms routinely earn large profits by trading as principal with customers, Investment Advisors cannot trade with clients as principal except in very limited and specific circumstances.
- Investment Advisors charge a pre-negotiated fee with their clients in advance of any transactions. They cannot earn additional profits or commissions from their customers' investments without prior consent. Registered Investment Advisors are commonly paid an asset-based fee that aligns their interests with those of their clients. Brokerage firms and stock brokers, on the other hand, have much different payment agreements. Their revenues may increase regardless of the performance of their customers' assets.
- Unlike brokerage firms, where investment banking and underwriting are commonplace, Registered Investment Advisors must manage money in the best interest of their customers. Because Registered Investment Advisors charge set fees for their services, their focus is on the client. Brokerage firms may focus on other aspects of the firm that do not contribute to the improvement of their clients' assets.
- Unlike brokers, Fee-Only Registered Investment Advisors do not get commissions from fund or insurance companies for selling their investment products.

Just to drive home the point, here is what a fiduciary duty to a client means for a Registered Investment Advisor. Registered Investment Advisors must:*
- Always act in the best interest of their client and make investment decisions that reflect their goals.

---

*2011 Advisor Sentiment Study, commissioned by TD AMERITRADE. TD Ameritrade, Inc.

- Identify and monitor securities that are illiquid (not easily converted to cash).
- When appropriate, employ fair market valuation procedures.
- Observe procedures regarding the allocation of investment opportunities, including new issues and the aggregation of orders.
- Have policies regarding affiliated broker-dealers and maintenance of brokerage accounts.
- Disclose all conflicts of interest.
- Have policies on use of brokerage commissions for research.
- Have policies regarding directed brokerage, including step-out trades and payment for order flow.
- Abide by a code of ethics.

CHAPTER 7 RECAP //

- Yellow Money may make Red Money less dangerous.
- Yellow Money is professionally managed.
- Yellow Money has a cohesive purpose and a strategy behind it
- If you haven't sat down and thought about how much money you need in order to generate income during retirement, you're just speculating.
- Red Money is like driving yourself in unfamiliar territory. With Yellow Money, you are still traveling by car, but now you have a professional driving on your behalf.
- Yellow Money is managed without emotions.
- Checking your truly Red Money should be like checking the sports section. You are interested in it, but it won't directly affect your lifestyle.

8

NEW IDEAS FOR INVESTING

In Chapter 1, we discussed how today's investment options require advice that is relevant to today. Traditional, outdated investment strategies are not only ineffective, they can be harmful to the average investor. One of the most traditional ways of thinking about investing is the risk versus reward trade-off. It goes something like this.

Investment options that are considered safer carry less risk, but also offer the potential for less return. Riskier investment options carry the burden of volatility and a greater potential for loss, but they also offer a greater potential for large rewards. Most professionals move their clients back and forth along this range, shifting between investments that are safer and investments that are structured for growth. Essentially, the old rules of investing dictate that you can either choose relative safety *or* return, but you can't have both.

Updated investment strategies work with the flexibility of liquidity to remake the rules. Here is how:

There are three dimensions that are inherent in any investment: *Liquidity, Safety,* and *Return.* You can maximize any two of these dimensions at the expense of the third. If you choose Safety and Liquidity, this is like keeping your assets in a checking account or savings account. This option delivers a lot of Safety and Liquidity, but at the expense of any Return. On the other hand, if you choose Liquidity and Return, meaning you have the potential for great return and can still reclaim your money whenever you choose, you will likely be exposed to a very high level of risk.

Understanding Liquidity can help you break the old Risk versus Safety trade-off. By identifying assets from which you don't require Liquidity, you can place yourself in a position to potentially profit from relatively safe investments that provide a higher than average rate of return.

Choosing Safety and Return over Liquidity can have significant impacts on the accumulation of your assets. In the following case, the paradigm shift from earning and saving to leveraging assets was a costly one.

> » *Ted is a corn and soybean farmer with 1,200 acres of land. He routinely retains somewhere between $40,000 and $80,000 in his checking and savings accounts. If a major piece of equipment fails and needs repair or replacement, Ted will need the money available to pay for the equipment and carry on with farming. If the price of feed for his cattle goes up one year, he will need to compensate for the increased overhead to his farming operation. He isn't a particularly wealthy farmer, but he has little choice but to keep a portion of money on hand in case something comes up and he must*

access it quickly. Most of his capital is held in livestock in the pasture or crops in the ground tied up for six to eight months of the year. When a major financial need arises, Ted can't just harvest 10 acres of soybeans and use them for payment. He needs to depend heavily on Liquidity in order to be a successful farmer.

Old habits die hard, however, and when Ted finally hangs up his overalls and quits farming, he keeps his bank accounts flush with cash, just like in the old days. After selling the farm and the equipment, Ted keeps a huge portion of the profits in Liquid investments because that's what he is familiar with. Unfortunately for Ted, with his pile of money sitting in his checking account, he isn't even keeping pace with inflation. After all his hard work as a farmer, his money is losing value every day because he didn't shift to a paradigm of leveraging his assets to generate income and accumulate value.

Almost anything would be a better option for Ted than clinging to Liquidity. He could have done something better to get either more return from his money or more safety, and at the very least would not have lost out to inflation.

As you can see, choosing Liquidity solely can be a costly option. The sooner you want your money back, the less you can leverage it for Safety or Return. If you have the option of putting your money in a long-term investment, you will be sacrificing Liquidity, but potentially gaining both Safety and Return. Rethinking your approach to money in this way can make a world of difference and can provide you with a structured way to generate income while allowing the value of your asset to grow over time.

The question is, how much Liquidity do you *really* need? Think about it. If you haven't sat down and created an income plan for your retirement, your perceived need for Liquidity is a guess. You don't know how much cash you'll need to fill the income gap if you don't know the amount of your Social Security benefit or the total of your other income options. If you *have* determined your income need and have made a plan for filling your income gap, you can partition your assets based on when you will need them. With an income plan in place, ***you can use new rules to enjoy both Safety and Return from your assets.***

CHAPTER 8 RECAP //

- Investment Advisors are obligated to make investment decisions or recommendations that are in your best interest and are aligned with your financial situation, timeframe and risk tolerance, and to put your interests ahead of their own. Stock brokers and brokerage firms are obligated to make suitable recommendations from the universe of products they are permitted to sell.

9
TAXES AND RETIREMENT

Taxes play a starring role in the theater of retirement planning. Everyone is familiar with taxes, but not everyone is familiar with how to make tax planning a part of their retirement strategy.

Taxes are taxes, right? You'll pay them before retirement and you'll pay them during retirement. What's the difference? The truth is that a planful approach to taxes can help you save money, protect your assets and ensure that your legacy remains intact.

How can a tax form do all that? The answer lies in planning. *Tax planning* and *tax reporting* are two very different things. Most people only *report* their taxes. March rolls around, people pull out their 1040s or use TurboTax to enter their income and taxable assets, and ship it off to Uncle Sam at the IRS. If you use a CPA to report your taxes, you are essentially paying them to record history. You have the option of being proactive with your taxes and to plan for your future by making smart, informed decisions about how taxes affect your overall financial plan. Working with a financial professional who, along with a CPA, makes recommendations about your finances to you, will keep you looking forward instead of in the rearview mirror as you enter retirement.

TAXES AND RETIREMENT

When you retire, you move from the earning and accumulation phase of your life into the asset distribution phase of your life. For most people, that means relying on Social Security, a 401(k), an IRA, or a pension. Wherever you have put your Green Money for retirement, you are going to start relying on it to provide you with the income that once came as a paycheck. Most of these distributions will be considered income by the IRS and will be taxed as such. There are exceptions to that (not all of your Social Security income is taxed, and income from Roth IRAs is not taxed), but for the most part, your distributions will be subject to income taxes.

Regarding assets that you have in an IRA, when you reach 70 ½ years of age, you will be required to draw a certain amount of money from your IRA as income each year. That amount depends on your age and the balance in your IRA. The amount that you are required to withdraw as income is called a Required Minimum Distribution (RMD). Why are you required to withdraw money from your own account? Chances are the money in that account has grown over time, and the government wants to collect taxes on that growth. If you have a large balance in an IRA, there's a chance your RMD could increase your income significantly enough to put you into a higher tax bracket, subjecting you to a higher incremental tax rate.

Here's where tax planning can really begin to work strongly in your favor. In the distribution phase of your life, you have a predictable income based on your RMDs, your Social Security benefit and any other income-generating assets you may have.

What really impacts you at this stage is how much of that money you keep in your pocket after taxes. If you can reduce your tax burden by 30, 20 or even 10 percent, you earn yourself that much more money by not paying it in taxes.

How do you save money on taxes? By having a plan. In this instance, a financial professional can work with the CPAs at their firm to create a **distribution plan** that minimizes your taxes and maximizes your annual net income.

BUILDING A TAX DIVERSIFIED PORTFOLIO

So far so good: avoid taxes, maximize your net annual income and have a plan for doing it. When people decide to leverage the experience and resources of a financial professional, they may not be thinking of how distribution planning and tax planning will benefit their portfolios. Often more exciting prospects like planning income annuities, investing in the market and structuring investments for growth rule the day. Taxes, however, play a crucial role in retirement planning. Achieving those tax goals requires knowledge of options, foresight and professional guidance.

Finding the path to a good tax plan isn't always a simple task. Every tax return you file is different from the one before it because things constantly change. Your expenses change. Planned or unplanned purchases occur. Health care costs, medical bills, an inheritance, property purchases, or reaching an age where your RMD kicks in are examples of any number of things that can affect how much income you report and how many deductions you take each year.

Preparing for the ever-changing landscape of your financial life requires a tax-diversified portfolio that can be leveraged to balance the incomes, expenditures and deductions that affect you each year. A financial professional will work with you to answer questions like these:

- What does your tax landscape look like?

- Do you have a tax-diversified portfolio robust enough to adapt to your needs?
- Do you have a diversity of taxable and non-taxable income planned for your retirement?
- Will you be able to maximize your distributions to take advantage of your deductions when you retire?
- Is your portfolio strong enough and tax-diversified enough to adapt to an ever-changing (and usually increasing) tax code?

» *When Darlene returns home after a week in the hospital recovering from a knee replacement, the 77-year-old calls her daughter, sister and brother to let them know she is home and feeling well. She also should have called her CPA. Darlene's medical expenses for the procedure, her hospital stay, her medications and the ongoing physical therapy she attended amount to $50,000.*

Currently, Americans age 65 and older can deduct medical expenses that are more than 75 percent of their Adjusted Gross Income (AGI). Darlene's AGI is $60,000 the year of her knee replacement, meaning she is able to deduct $45,500 of her medical bills from her taxes that year ($50,000 - [$60,000 x .075]). Her AGI dictated that she could deduct more than 75 percent of her medical expenses that year. Darlene didn't know this.

Had she been working with a financial professional who regularly asked her about any changes in her life, her spending, or her expenses (expected or unexpected), Darlene could have saved thousands of dollars. Darlene can also file an amendment to her tax return to recoup the overpayment.

This relatively simple example of how tax planning can save you money is just the tip of the iceberg. No one can be expected to know the entire U.S. tax code. But a professional who is working with a team of CPAs and financial professionals have an advantage over the average taxpayer who must start from square one on their own every year. Have you been taking advantage of all the deductions that are available to you?

PROACTIVE TAX PLANNING

The implications of proactive tax planning are far reaching, and are larger than many people realize. Remember, doing your taxes in January, February, March or April means you are writing a history book. Planning your taxes in October, November or December means that you are writing the story as it happens. You can look at all the factors that are at play and make decisions that will impact your tax return *before* you file it.

Realizing that tax planning is an aspect of financial planning is an important leap to make. When you incorporate tax planning into your financial planning strategy, it becomes part of the way you maximize your financial potential. Paying less in taxes means you keep more of your money. Simply put, the more money you keep, the more of it you can leverage as an asset. This kind of planning can affect you at any stage of your life. If you are 40 years old, are you contributing the maximum amount to your 401(k) plan? Are you contributing to a Roth IRA? Are you finding ways to structure the savings you are dedicating to your children's education? Do you have life insurance? Taxes and tax planning affect all of these investment tools. Having a relationship with a professional who works with a CPA can help you build a truly comprehensive financial plan that not only works with your investments, but also shapes your assets to find the most efficient ways to prepare for tax time. There may be years that you could benefit from higher distributions because of the tax bracket that you are in, or there could be years you would benefit from taking less. There may be years when you have a lot of deductions and years you have relatively few. Adapting your distributions to work in concert with your available deductions is at the heart of smart tax planning. Professional guidance can bring you to the next level of income distribution, allowing you to remain flexible enough to maximize your tax efficiency. And remember, saving money on taxes makes you more money than making money does.

What you have on paper is important: your assets, savings, investments, which are the financial expression of your work and time. It's just as important to know how to get it off the paper in a way that keeps most of it in your pocket. Almost anything that involves financial planning also involves taxes. Annuities, investments, IRAs, 401(k)s, 403(b)s, and many other investment options will have tax implications. Life also has a way of throwing curveballs. Illness, expensive car repairs or replacement, or *any event that has a financial impact on your life will likely have a corresponding tax implication* around which you should adapt your financial plan. Tax planning does just that.

One dollar can end up being less than 25 cents to your heirs.

> » *When Peter's father passed away, he discovered that he was the beneficiary of his father's $500,000 IRA. Peter has a wife and a family of four children, and he knew that his father had intended for a large portion of the IRA to go toward funding their college educations.*
>
> *After Peter's father's estate is distributed, Peter, who is 50 years old and whose two oldest sons are entering college, liquidates the IRA. By doing so, his taxable income for that year puts him in a 39.6 percent tax bracket, immediately reducing the value of the asset to $302,000. An additional 3.8 percent surtax on net investment income further diminishes the funds to $283,000. Liquidating the IRA in effect subjects much of*

Peter's regular income to the surtax, as well. At this point, Peter will be taxed at 43.4 percent.

Peter's state taxes are an additional 9 percent. Moreover, estate taxes on Peter's father's assets claim another 22 percent. By the time the IRS is through, Peter's income from the IRA will be taxed at 75 percent, leaving him with $125,000 of the original $500,000. While it would help contribute to the education of his children, it wouldn't come anywhere near completely paying for it, something the $500,000 could have easily done. Working with an expert, experienced retirement planner could have helped Peter make more sense of his situation.

As the above example makes clear, leaving an asset to your beneficiaries can be more complicated than it may seem. In the case of a traditional IRA, after federal, estate and state taxes, the asset could literally diminish to as little as 25 percent of its value.

How does working with a professional help you make smarter tax decisions with your own finances? Any financial professional worth their salt will be working with a firm that has a team of trained tax professionals, including CPAs, who have an intimate knowledge of the tax code and how to adapt a financial plan to it.

Here's another example of how taxes have major implications on asset management:

» Greg and Rhonda, a 62-year-old couple, begin working with a financial professional in October. After structuring their assets to reflect their risk tolerance and creating assets that would provide them Green Money income during retirement, they feel good about their situation. They make decisions that allow them to maximize their Social Security benefits, they have plenty of options for filling their income gap, and have begun a safe yet ambitious Yellow Money strategy with their

professional. When their professional asks them about their tax plan, they tell him their CPA handled their taxes every year, and did a great job. Their professional says, "I don't mean who does your taxes, I mean, who does your tax planning?" Greg and Rhonda aren't sure how to respond.

Their professional brings Greg and Rhonda's financial plan to the firm's CPA and has her run a tax projection for them. A week later their professional calls them with a tax plan for the year that will save them more than $3,000 on their tax return. The couple is shocked. A simple piece of advice from the CPA based on the numbers revealed that if they paid their estimated taxes before the end of the year, they would be able to itemize it as a deduction, allowing them to save thousands of dollars.

This solution won't work for everyone, and it may not work for Greg and Rhonda every year. That's not the point. By being proactive with their approach to taxes and using the resources made available by their financial professional, they were able to create a tax plan that saved them money.

YELLOW MONEY AND TAXES

There are also tax implications for the money that you have managed professionally. People with portions of their investment portfolio that are actively traded can particularly benefit from having a proactive tax strategy. Without going into too much detail, for tax purposes there are two kinds of investment money: qualified and non-qualified. Different investment strategies can have different effects on how you are taxed on your investments and the growth of your investments. Some are more beneficial for one kind of investment strategy over another. Determining how to plan for the taxation of non-qualified and qualified investments is fodder for holiday party discussions at accounting firms. While it may not be a stimulating topic for the average investor, you don't have to understand exactly how it works in order to benefit from it.

While there are many differences between qualified and non-qualified investments, the main difference is this: qualified plans are designed to give investors tax benefits by deferring taxation of their growth until they are withdrawn. Non-qualified investments are not eligible for these deferral benefits. As such, non-qualified investments are taxed whenever income is realized from them in the form of growth.

Actively and non-actively traded investments provide a simple example of how to position your investments for the best tax advantage. In an actively traded and managed portfolio, there is a high amount of buying and selling of stocks, bonds, funds, ETFs, etc. If that active portfolio of non-qualified investments does well and makes a 20 percent return one year and you are in the 39.6 percent tax bracket, your net gain from that portfolio is only about 12 percent (39.6 percent tax of the 20 percent gain is roughly 8 percent.) In a passive trading strategy, you can use a qualified investment tool, such as an IRA, to achieve 13, 14 or 15 percent growth (much lower than the actively traded portfolio), but still realize a higher net return because the growth of the qualified investment is not taxed until it is withdrawn.

Does this mean that you have to always rely on a buy and hold strategy in qualified investment tools? Not necessarily. The question is, if you have qualified and non-qualified investments, where do you want to position your actively traded and managed assets? Incorporating a planful approach to positioning your investments for more beneficial taxation can be done many ways, but let's consider one example. Keeping your actively managed investment strategies inside an IRA or some other qualified plan could allow you to realize the higher gains of those investments without paying tax on their growth every year. Your more passively managed funds could then be kept in taxable, non-qualified vehicles and methods, and because you aren't realizing income from them on an annual basis by frequently trading them, they grow sheltered from taxation.

If you are interested in taking advantage of tax strategies that maximize your net income, you need the attentive strategies, experience and knowledge of a professional who can give you options that position you for profit. At the end of the day, what's important to you as the consumer is how much of your after tax income you retain.

ESTATE TAXES

The government doesn't just tax your income from investments while you're alive. They will also dip into your legacy.

While estate taxes aren't as hot of a topic as they were a few years ago, they are still an issue of concern for many people with assets. While taxes may not apply on estates that are less than $5 million, certain states have estate taxes with much lower exclusion ratios. Some are as low as $600,000. Many people may have to pay a state estate tax. One strategy for avoiding those types of taxes is to move assets outside of your estate. That can include gifting them to family or friends, or putting them into an irrevocable trust. Life insurance is another option for protecting your legacy. Seek a retirement planning expert and an estate planning attorney for guidance.

10

THE FUTURE OF U.S. TAXATION

A derivation of the phrase, "Nothing is certain except for death and taxes" has been around since even before the nation's first taxes were levied, and it continues to ring true today. However, due to recent upheavals in the American financial landscape, this saying might need to be modified to, "nothing is certain except for death and increasing taxes."

Since June 25, 1940, the debt ceiling has been raised 93 times, which represents an average debt limit increase of roughly 1.3 times per year. With the well-being of our economy in jeopardy, legislation regarding debt reduction and tax reform has become a hot button issue. Regardless of which legislation has been, or will be, thrown at us, the truth of the matter remains the same: our current tax revenues cannot cover our obligations.

If our government wants to keep the lights on, it is going to need more income, which not only means that you can count on being taxed, but also on being taxed at an increasing rate.

DEBT CEILING – CAUSE AND EFFECTS

The continual increasing of the debt ceiling has raised more than just the ability for our government to go further into debt; it has raised concerns and fears about the future of our economy. We continue to see major swings in the markets with investors showing serious concerns over the future of investment valuations and their personal wealth. As the debate surrounding our national debt wages on, it is clear that some degree of tax reform is, and will be, required in order to correct the underlying problems that have made raising the debt ceiling necessary.

Increasing the debt ceiling is needed because the government keeps maxing out its credit limit, which it has been reliant upon since the Industrial Revolution began. The government's tendency to spend beyond its means is really not much different than what the general public has been doing for the past few decades as well. However, most people do not have the ability to get a credit limit increase on a credit line that has already reached its maximum limit, unless they can show they have the ability to pay the balance back, which means they need to show that the amount of money they're making is more than the amount of money they're spending. In other words, they need to show they have a balanced budget.

The federal government keeps finding ways to increase its credit line without also finding ways to proportionally cut its spending. To get things back in balance, the government is in desperate need of finding ways to decrease its spending and make more money. Although legislation has been put in place to give the appearance of spending cuts through future sequestration, the politicians in charge often still find a way to reduce these cuts.

Consequently, the only way for the government to compensate for its lack of spending cuts is by making more money. However, the only way the government makes money is by collecting taxes. Unfortunately, at the current moment, the government collects approximately $42 billion less per month than it spends*.

DEBT AND EARNINGS

Let us take a closer look at where we are today. The national debt is increasing at an unprecedented rate, rising to levels never seen before and threatening serious harm to the economy. In October 2004, the national debt was $7.4 trillion**, and by October 2014 it had climbed to $17.9 trillion***, which means the national debt grew 241.9 percent during this 10 year time period or 8.4percent annually compounded. That being said, the national debt's annual growth rate has receded significantly over the past three years, falling to an annual growth rate of 4.5 percent.

To put this into perspective, the national gross domestic product (GDP) through the third quarter 2014 was approximately $17.5 trillion****, up from $12.3 trillion in 2004. As of the end of 2011, the last time this paper was updated, the national debt level was 95.3 percent of GDP. Economists believe that a sustainable economy exists at a maximum level of approximately 80 percent. Today, the U.S. national debt is 101.8 percent of the GDP*****.

The significance of these two numbers lies within the contrast. The national debt is the amount that needs to be repaid; this can be thought of as the government's credit balance. Gross domestic

---

* Congressional Budget Office projected deficit baseline 2014 - 2024

** CBO, An Update to the Budget and Economic Outlook: 2014 - 2024

*** US Department of the Treasury's Bureau of the Fiscal Service, www.treasurydirect. gov/NP/debt/current

**** US Department of Commerce's Bureau of Economic Analysis, National Income and Product Accounts Tables

***** Federal Reserve Bank of St Louis Economic Research

product (GDP) represents the market value of all final goods and services produced within a country during a given period. Essentially, GDP represents the gross taxable income available to the government. If debts are increasing at a rate greater than the gross income available for taxation, then the only way to make up the difference is to increase the rate at which the gross income is being taxed.

As previously mentioned, and as the most recent analysis by the Congressional Budget Office (CBO) shows, the deficit's growth rate has recently declined significantly and is projected to continue to decline through 2015, before once again beginning to increase at an unprecedented rate. However, both this report and the 2015 Presidential Budget show a continuing trend in disparity between the national debt and GDP over the next decade. Borrowing more money than you make on a continuous basis is an epic disaster lying in wait.

Although this increasing disparity is a real concern and shows that, at least in the short run, the federal deficit will not be addressed to counteract the apparently inevitable crisis ahead, it is the revenue collection that tells the most disconcerting story. Over the past 40 years, the average collection of GDP for revenue has been approximately 17.3 percent, which is approximately where collections lie today.

To offer some perspective on the collection rate, consider the fact that collections were at 14.4 percent in 2012. Since that point there have been several different tax increases, and the recent Roth conversion limitation removals have gone into effect, which helps explain the increase in collections.

As the presidential budget reveals, the projected revenues are estimated to be approximately 19.2 percent by the end of the next decade. That is an 11 percent increase in the revenue rate which, when related to the current tax rates, would put someone currently in the 39.6 percent tax bracket into the 44 percent tax bracket. The reality of this increase means that additional tax increases are on the horizon, and it would appear that this is going to be a graduated process beginning in 2015. Consequently, the debt ceiling discussions will most likely be accompanied by a plan to implement additional tax increases that will occur over a period of three to five years.

Unfortunately, the budget also shows that regardless of revenue collection rates and increased taxes, the deficit is going to continue to increase. Sadly, without additional spending cuts to bring the budget into balance, we will continue to see tax increases over the coming years beyond this budget.

THE END OF AN ERA

From a historical point of view, taxes are extremely low. The last time the U.S. national debt was even close to the same percentage level of GDP as it is today was at the end of World War II and for several years following. The maximum tax rate at that point, and through the years from 1944 through 1963, averaged 90 percent. Compare that to the maximum rate of 39.6 percent today, and it becomes very clear that there is a disparity of extreme proportion.

Taxes during this historical period were at extreme levels for nearly 20 years, during and following this level of debt-to-GDP. A significant point to note about the difference at that time versus where we are today is the economic activity.

The period of 1944 through 1963 was in the heart of both the Industrial Revolution and the birth of the baby-boom generation. Today, we are mired in extreme volatility with frequent periods of boom and bust accompanied by the beginning of the greatest retirement wave ever experienced within the U.S. economy.

To contrast these two time periods in respect to the recovery period is almost asinine as the external pressures from globalization and domestic unfunded liabilities did not exist or were irrelevant factors during the prior period.

To add insult to injury, U.S. domestic unfunded liabilities were estimated to be about $84 trillion in 2012 and that number has only increased through the intervening years*. These liabilities exist outside of the annual budgetary debt discussed above and are due to items such as Social Security, Medicare and government pensions. The most concerning part of this goes back to the previous discussion of being on the cusp of the greatest retirement wave in U.S. history as the baby-boom generation begins retiring and expiring the unfunded Social Security for which they currently have entitlement. Over the long-run, expenditures related to healthcare programs such as Medicare and Medicaid are projected to grow faster than the economy overall as the population matures.

To put unfunded liabilities into perspective, consider these as off-balance-sheet obligations similar to those of Enron. Although these are not listed as part of the national debt, they must be paid just the same. The difference between Enron and the U.S. unfunded liabilities is that if the U.S. government cannot come up with the funds to pay all these liabilities through revenue generation then they will print the money necessary to pay the debt.

WHAT DOES THE SOLUTION LOOK LIKE?

Unfortunately, the general public is in a no-win situation for this solution to the problem. Printing money does not bode well for economic growth as this action creates inflationary pressures that devalue the U.S. dollar and make everyone less wealthy. Cutting the entitlements that compose this liability leaves millions of people with fewer benefits than they have come to expect. The only other option, and one that the government knows all too well, is increased taxes. In fact, according to a Congressional

---

National Center for Policy Analysis, How Much Does the Federal Government Owe?, June 2012

Budget Office paper issued in 2004*, unfunded liabilities are addressed as follows:

"The term 'unfunded liability' has been used to refer to a gap between the government's projected financial commitment under a particular program and the revenues that are expected to be available to fund that commitment. But no government obligation can be truly considered 'unfunded' because of the U.S. government's sovereign power to tax—which is the ultimate resource to meet its obligations."

A balanced budget is going to be required at some point and with this will come higher taxes. Given our current position and projected budgets, it is fairly safe to say that tax increases are coming in the near future. And as we continue to aspire in insanity by doing the same things over and over while expecting different results we will find that raising taxes is a strategy to raise money, but it is not a solution to our current and pending problems.

You make more money by saving on taxes than you do by making more money. The simplistic logic of that statement really makes sense when you discover it takes a $1.50 in earnings to put that same dollar, saved in taxes, back into your pocket**. This simple concept becomes extremely valuable to people in retirement and those living on fixed incomes.

As simple as it sounds, it is much more difficult to execute. Most people fail to put together a plan as they near retirement, beginning with a simple cash flow budget. If we have not analyzed our proposed income streams and expenses, we could not possibly have taken the time to position these cash flows and other events into a tax-preferred plan.

Most people will state, "I have a plan" and thus, they do not need any further assistance in this area. The truth in most in-

---

*CBO paper, *Measures of the U.S. Government's Fiscal Position Under Current Law,* Sept. 2004

**Assuming a 33 percent effective tax rate

stances is that people could not show you their plan, and of the few that could, they would not be able to show you how they have executed it. In this regard, they may as well be Richard Nixon stating, "I am not a crook" for as much as they state, "I have a plan." The truth lies in waiting.

As you approach or begin retirement, you should look at what cash flows you will have. Do you have a pension? How about Social Security? How much additional cash flow are you going to need to draw from your assets to maintain the lifestyle that you desire?

We spend our whole lives saving and accumulating wealth but very little time determining how to distribute this accumulation to keep it. We need to make sure we have the appropriate diversification of taxable versus non-taxable assets to complement our distribution strategy.

THE BENEFITS OF DIVERSIFICATION

Heading into retirement, you should be situated with a diversified tax landscape. The point to spending your whole life accumulating wealth is not to see how big the number is on paper, but rather, it should be an exercise in how much you put in your pocket after removing it from the paper.

To truly understand tax diversification, you must understand what types of money exist and how each of these will be treated during accumulation and, most importantly, during distribution. The following is a brief summary:

Free money
  1. Tax-free money
  2. Tax-deferred money
  3. Taxable money
      a. Ordinary income
      b. Capital gains and qualified dividends

FREE MONEY

Free money is the best kind of money regardless of the tax treatment, because in the end you have more money than you would have otherwise. Many employers will provide contributions toward employee retirement accounts to offer additional employment benefits and inspire employees to save for their own retirement. With this, employers often times will offer a matching contribution in which they will contribute up to a certain percentage of an employee's salary, generally three to five percent, to that employee's retirement account when the employee contributes to their retirement account as well. For example, if an employee earns $50,000 annually and contributes three percent ($1,500) to their retirement account annually, the employer will also contribute three percent ($1,500) to the employee's account. That is $1,500 in free money. Take all that you can get!

TAX-FREE MONEY

Tax-free money is the next best thing to free-money. Although you have to earn tax-free money you do not have to give part of it away to Uncle Sam. Tax-free money comes in three basic forms that you can utilize during your lifetime; four if prison inspires your future, but we are not going to discuss that option.

The most commonly known form of tax-free money is municipal bonds, which earn and pay interest that could be federally tax-free, state tax-free, or both state and federal tax-free. There are several caveats that should be discussed in regard to the notion of tax-free income from municipal bonds. First, you will notice that tax-free has several flavors from the state and federal perspective. This is because states will generally tax the interest earned on a municipal bond unless the bond is offered from an entity located within that state. This severely limits the availability of completely tax-free municipal bonds and constrains underlying risk and liquidity factors. Second, municipal bond interest gets added back into the equation for determining your modified adjusted gross income (MAGI) for Social Security and could push your income above the thresholds subjecting a portion of your Social Security income to taxation. In effect, if this interest subjects some other income to taxation then this interest is truly being taxed. Last, municipal bond interest may be excluded from the regular federal tax system, but it is included for determining tax under the alternative minimum tax (AMT) system. I will not go into details on what the alternative minimum tax system is here, but the one thing everyone should know about AMT is that it is bad. In its basic form, the AMT system is a separate tax system that applies if the tax computed under AMT exceeds the tax computed under the regular tax system, the difference between these two computations is the alternative minimum tax.

TAX-FREE MONEY: ROTH IRA

Roth accounts are probably the single greatest tax asset that has come from Congress outside of life insurance and are well known of, but rarely used. Roth IRAs were first established by the Taxpayer Relief Act of 1997 and named after Senator William Roth, the chief sponsor of the legislation. Roth accounts are simply a retirement account that can be in the form of an individual retirement account or an employer sponsored retirement account that allow for tax-free growth of earnings and tax-free income.

The main difference between a Roth and a traditional IRA or employer sponsored plan lies within the timing of the taxation. We are all very familiar with the typical scenario of putting money away for retirement through an employer plan, whereby they deduct money from our paychecks and put it directly into a retirement account. This money is taken out before taxes are calculated so we do not pay tax on those earnings today. A Roth account on the other hand takes the money after the taxes have been taken out and then puts it into the retirement account, so we do pay tax on the money today. The other significant difference between these two is taxation during distribution in later years. With our traditional retirement accounts when we take the money out later it gets added to our ordinary income and gets taxed accordingly. Additionally, by including this in our income it subjects us to such things mentioned above for municipal bonds with Social Security taxation, AMT, as well as higher Medicare premiums. A Roth on the other hand gets distributed tax-free and does not contribute toward negative impact items such as Social Security taxation, AMT, or Medicare premium increases. It essentially comes back to us without tax and other obligations, as they've been paid for upfront on the initial Roth investment.

The best way to view the difference between the two accounts is to look at the life of a farmer. A farmer will buy seed, plant it in the ground, grow the crops, and harvest it later for sale. Typically, the farmer would only pay tax on the crops that have been harvested and sold. Let me ask the question however, if you were the farmer, would you rather pay tax on $5,000 worth of seed that you plant today or $50,000 worth of harvested crop later? The obvious answer is $5,000 worth of seed today. The truth to the matter is that you are a farmer, only you plant dollars into your retirement account instead of seeds into the earth.

So why doesn't everyone have a Roth retirement account if things are so simple? There are several reasons, but the single greatest reason has been the constraints on contributions. If you earned over certain thresholds (MAGI over $129,000 single and $191,000 joint for 2014), you were not eligible to make contributions, and until 2010 if your modified adjusted gross income (MAGI) was over $100,000 (single or joint) then you could not convert a traditional to a Roth. Outside of these contribution limits, most people save for retirement through their employers and most employers are not offering Roth options within their plans. The reason behind this is because Roth accounts are not that well understood and people have been educated to believe that saving on taxes today is the best possible course of action.

TAX-FREE MONEY: LIFE INSURANCE

As I previously mentioned, the single greatest tax asset that has come from Congress outside of life insurance is the Roth account. Life insurance is the little known or discussed tax asset that holds some of the greatest value for our financial lives both during life and upon death and is by far the best tax-free device available. We traditionally view life insurance as a way to protect our loved ones from financial ruin upon our demise and it should be noted that everyone who cares about someone should have life insurance. By purchasing a life insurance policy our loved ones will be assured a financial windfall from the life insurance company when we die to help them with our final expenses and carry on their lives without us comfortably. The best part about the life insurance windfall is the fact that nobody will have to pay tax on the money received. This is the single greatest tax-free device available, but it has one downside, we do not get to use it … only our heirs will.

The little known and discussed part of life insurance is the cash value build-up within whole life and universal life (permanent) policies. Life insurance is not typically seen as an investment vehicle for building wealth and retirement planning, although we should discuss briefly why this thought process should be re-evaluated. Permanent life insurance is generally misconceived as something that is very expensive for a wealth accumulation vehicle as there are mortality charges (fees for the death benefit) that detract from the returns that are available and further, those returns do not yield as much as the stock market over the long run. This is why many times you will hear the phrase "buy term and invest the rest," where "term" refers to term insurance.

Let us take just a second to review two terms just used in regard to life insurance: term and permanent.

Term insurance is what most people are familiar with, you purchase a certain death benefit that will go to your heirs upon your death and this policy will be in effect for a certain number of years, typically 10 to 20 years. The 10 to 20 years is the term of the policy and once we have reached that end we no longer have insurance unless we purchase another policy at that point.

Permanent insurance on the other hand has no term involved, it is permanent as long as the premiums continue to be paid. Permanent insurance generally has higher premiums than term insurance for the same amount of death benefit coverage and it is this difference that is referred to when people say "invest the rest."

Simply speaking there are significant differences between these two policies that do not get taken into consideration when providing a comparative analysis in the numbers. One item that gets lost in the fray when comparing term and permanent insurance is that term usually expires before death, in fact insurance studies show less than 1 percent of all term policies pay out death benefit claims. The issue arises when the term expires and the desire to have more insurance is still present. A term policy with the same benefit will be much more expensive than the original policy and many times life events occur with illness such as cancer or heart conditions that make it impossible to acquire another policy, leaving our loved ones unprotected and tax-free legacy planning out of the equation.

Another aspect and probably the most important piece in consideration of the future of taxation is the fact that permanent insurance has a cash accumulation value. Two aspects stand out with the cash accumulation value. First, as the cash accumulation value increases the death benefit will also increase where term insurance is level. Second, this cash accumulation offers value to you during your lifetime rather than just your heirs upon death. The cash accumulation value can be used for tax-free income during your lifetime through policy loans. Most importantly, this tax-free income is available during retirement for distribution planning, all while offering the same typical financial protection to your heirs.

TAX-DEFERRED MONEY

Tax-deferred money is the type of money from which most of us are familiar and has been reviewed briefly already, so I will not spend much time reviewing them here. Tax-deferred money is typically our traditional IRA, employer sponsored retirement plan, or a non-qualified annuity. Essentially we put money into an investment vehicle that will accumulate in value over time and we do not pay taxes on the earnings that grow these accounts until we distribute them. Once the money is distributed taxes must be paid and in addition to the taxes, the same negative consequences exist toward additional taxation and expense in other areas as previously discussed.

TAXABLE MONEY

Taxable money is everything else and is taxable both today and later, whenever it is received. Of these four types of money, they really come down to two distinct classifications; taxable and tax-free. The greatest difference between taxable and tax-free income is a function of how much money we keep after tax. For help in determining what the differences should be, exclusive of outside factors such as Social Security taxation and AMT, a tax equivalent yield should be used.

TAX-FREE IN THE REAL WORLD

To put the tax equivalent yield into perspective, let us look at an example:

> » Bob and Mary are currently retired and in the 25 percent
> tax bracket living on Social Security and interest from invest-

ments. They have a substantial portion of their investments in municipal bonds yielding 6.0 percent, which in today's market is quite comforting. The tax equivalent yield they would need to earn from a taxable investment would be 8.0 percent, a 2.0 percent gap which seems almost impossible given current market volatility. However, something that has never been put into perspective is that the interest from their municipal bonds is subject to taxation on their Social Security benefits* (at 21.25 percent). With this, the yield on their municipal bonds would be 4.725 percent**, and the taxable equivalent yield falls to 6.3 percent leaving a gap of only 1.575 percent.

In the end, most people spend their lives accumulating wealth through the best, if not only vehicle they know, a tax-deferred account. This account is most likely a 401(k) or 403(b) plan offered through their employer and may be supplemented with an IRA that was established at one point or another. As the years go by, people blindly throw money into these accounts in an effort to save for a retirement that they someday hope to reach.

The truth is most people have an age selected for when they would like to retire but many of them spend their lives wondering if they will ever be able to actually quit working. To answer this question, you must understand how much money you will have available to contribute toward your needs. In other words, you need to know what your after-tax income will be during this period.

All else being equal, it would not matter if you put your money into a taxable, tax-deferred, or tax-free account as long as income tax rates never change and outside factors are never an event. The

---

**Assuming each dollar of interest subjects a dollar of Social Security income to taxation at 85 percent*

***6.0 percent – (6.0 percent -21.25 percent) = 4.725 percent*

net amount you receive in the end will be the same. Unfortunately, none of this will ever be the circumstance. We already know that taxes will increase in the future with the likely forecast of being higher in retirement than during our peak earning years.

Regardless, saving for retirement in any form is a good thing since it appears from all practical perspectives that future government benefits will be cut and taxes will increase. You have the ability to plan today for efficient tax diversification and maximization of your after-tax dollars during your distribution years.

11

THE BRANDEIS STORY

Louis Brandeis provides one of the best examples illustrating how tax planning works. Brandeis was Associate Justice on the Supreme Court of the United States from 1916 to 1939. Born in Louisville, Kentucky, Brandeis was an intelligent man with a touch of country charm. He described tax planning this way:

"I live in Alexandria, Virginia. Near the Court Chambers, there is a toll bridge across the Potomac. When in a rush, I pay the dollar toll and get home early. However, I usually drive outside the downtown section of the city and cross the Potomac on a free bridge.

The bridge was placed outside the downtown Washington, D.C. area to serve a useful social service—getting drivers to drive the extra mile and help alleviate congestion during the rush hour.

If I went over the toll bridge and through the barrier without paying a toll, I would be committing tax evasion.

If I drive the extra mile and drive outside the city of Washington to the free bridge, I am using a legitimate, logical and suitable method of tax avoidance, and I am performing a useful social service by doing so.

*The tragedy is that few people **know that the free bridge exists.**"*

Like Brandeis, most American taxpayers have options when it comes to "crossing the Potomac," so to speak. It's a financial planner's job to tell you what options are available. You can wait until March to file your taxes, at which time you might pay someone to report and pay the government a larger portion of your income. However, you could instead file before the end of the year, work with your financial professional and incorporate a tax plan as part of your overall financial planning strategy. Filing later is like crossing the toll bridge. Tax planning is like crossing the free bridge.

Which would you rather do?

The answer to this question is easy. Most people want to save money and pay less in taxes. What makes this situation really difficult in real life, however, is that the signs along the side of the road that direct us to the free bridge are not that clear. To normal Americans, and to plenty of people who have studied it, the U.S. tax code is confusing. There are all kinds of rules, exceptions to rules, caveats and conditions that are difficult to know about or understand. You really need to know your options and the bottom line impacts of those options.

ROTH IRA CONVERSIONS

The attractive qualities of Roth IRAs may have prompted you to explore the possibility of moving some of your assets into a Roth account. Another important difference between the accounts is how they treat Required Minimum Distributions (RMDs). When you turn 70 ½ years old, you are required to take a minimum amount of money out of a traditional IRA. This amount is your

RMD. It is treated as taxable income. Roth IRAs, however, do not have RMDs, and their distributions are not taxable. Quite a deal, right?

While having a Roth IRA as part of your portfolio is a good idea, converting assets to a Roth IRA can pose some challenges, depending on what kinds of assets you want to transfer.

One common option is the conversion of a traditional IRA to a Roth IRA. You may have heard about converting your IRA to a Roth IRA, but you might not know the full net result on your income. The main difference between the two accounts is that the growth of investments within a traditional IRA is not taxed until income is withdrawn from the account, whereas taxes are charged on contribution amounts to a Roth IRA, not withdrawals. The problem, however, is that when assets are removed from a traditional IRA, even if the assets are being transferred to a Roth IRA account, taxes apply.

There are a lot of reasons to look at Roth conversions. People have a lot of money in IRAs, up to multiple millions of dollars. Even with $500,000, when they turn 70.5 years old, their RMD is going to be approximately $18,000, and they have to take that out whether they want to or not. It's a tax issue. Essentially, if you will be subject to high RMDs, it could have impacts on how much of your Social Security is taxable, and on your tax bracket.

By paying taxes now instead of later on assets in a Roth IRA, you can realize tax-advantaged growth. You pay once and you're done paying. Your heirs are done paying. It's a powerful tool. Here's a simple example to show you how powerful it can be:

Imagine that you pay to convert a traditional IRA to a Roth. You have decided that you want to put the money in a vehicle that gives you a tax-advantaged income option down the road. If you pay a 25 percent tax on that conversion and the Roth IRA then doubles in value over the next 10 years, you could look at your situation as only having paid 12.5 percent tax.

The prospect of tax-advantaged income is a tempting one. While you have to pay a conversion tax to transfer your assets, you also have turned taxable income into tax free retirement money that you can let grow as long as you want without being required to withdraw it.

There are options, however, that address this problem. Much like the Brandeis story, there may be a "free bridge" option for many investors.

Your financial professional will likely tell you that it is not a matter of whether or not you should perform a Roth IRA conversion, it is a matter of how much you should convert and when.

Here are some of the things to consider before converting to a Roth IRA:

- If you make a conversion before you retire, you may end up paying higher taxes on the conversion because it is likely that you are in some of your highest earning years, placing you in the highest tax bracket of your life. It is possible that a better strategy would be to wait until after you retire, a time when you may have less taxable income, which would place you in a lower tax bracket.
- Many people opt to reduce their work hours from full-time to part-time in the years before they retire. If you have pursued this option, your income will likely be lower, in turn lowering your tax rate.
- The first years that you draw Social Security benefits can also be years of lower reported income, making it another good time frame in which to convert to a Roth IRA.

One key strategy to handling a Roth IRA conversion is to always be able to pay the cost of the tax conversion with outside money. Structuring your tax year to include something like a significant deduction can help you offset the conversion tax. This way you aren't forced to take the money you need for taxes from the value of the IRA. The reason taxes apply to this maneuver is because when you withdraw money from a traditional IRA, it is treated as taxable income by the IRS. Your financial professional, with the help of the CPAs at their firm, may be able to provide you with options like after-tax money, itemized deductions or other situations that can pose effective tax avoidance options.

Some examples of avoiding Roth IRA conversions taxes include:

- Using medical expenses that are greater than 10 percent of your Adjusted Gross Income. If you have health care costs that you can list as itemized deductions, you can convert an amount of income from a traditional IRA to a Roth IRA that is offset by the deductible amount. Essentially, deductible medical expenses negate the taxes resulting from recording the conversion.
- *Individuals, usually small business owners, who are dealing with a Net Operating Loss (NOL).* If you have NOLs, but aren't able to utilize all of them on your tax return. You can carry them forward to offset the taxable income from the taxes on income you convert to a Roth IRA.
- Charitable giving. If you are charitably inclined, you can use the amount of your donations to reduce the amount of taxable income you have during that year. By matching the amount you convert to a Roth IRA to the amount your taxable income was reduced by charitable giving, you can essentially avoid taxation on the conversion. You may decide to double your donations to a charity in one year, giving them two years' worth of donations in order to offset the Roth IRA conversion tax on this year's tax return.
- Investments that are subject to depletion. Certain investments can kick off depletion expenses. If you make an

investment and are subject to depletion expenses, they can be deducted and used to offset a Roth IRA conversion tax.

Not all of the above scenarios work for everyone, and there are many other options for offsetting conversion taxes. The point is that you have options, and your financial professional and tax professional can help you understand those options.

If you have a traditional IRA, Roth conversions are something you should look at. As you approach retirement you should consider your options and make choices that keep more of your money in your pocket, not the government's.

ADDITIONAL TAX BENEFITS OF ROTH IRAS

Not only do Roth IRAs provide you with tax-advantaged growth, they also give you a tax diversified landscape that allows you to maximize your distributions. Chances are that no matter the circumstances, you will have taxed income and other assets subject to taxation. *If you have a Roth IRA, you have the unique ability to manage your Adjusted Gross Income (AGI), because you have a tax-advantaged income option!*

Converting to a Roth IRA can also help you preserve and build your legacy because Roth IRAs are exempt from RMDs. If you make a conversion from a traditional IRA, your Roth account can grow tax-advantaged for another 15, 20 or 25 years and it can be used as tax-advantaged income by your heirs. It is important to note, however, that non-spousal beneficiaries do have to take RMDs from a Roth IRA, or choose to stretch it and draw tax-advantaged income out of it over their lifetime. It is important to note that you must have a Roth IRA for five years in order to withdraw earnings tax-free and you can only contribute/rollover a maximum of $6,500 per year if over the age of 50.

TO CONVERT OR NOT TO CONVERT?

Conversions aren't only for retirees. You can convert at any time. Your choice should be based on your individual circumstances and tax situation. Sticking with a traditional IRA or converting to a Roth, depends on your individual circumstances, including your income, your tax bracket and the amount of deductions you have each year.

Is it better to have a Roth IRA or traditional IRA? It depends on your individual circumstances. Some people don't mind having taxable income from an IRA. Their income might not be very high and their RMD might not bump their tax bracket up, so it's not a big deal. A similar situation might involve income from Social Security. Social Security benefits are taxed based on other income you are drawing. If you are in a position where none or very little of your Social Security benefit is subject to taxes, paying income tax on your RMD may be very easy.

> » *There are also situations where leveraging taxable income from a traditional IRA can work to your advantage come tax time. For example, Darrel and Linda dream of buying a boat when they retire. It is something they have looked forward to during their entire marriage. In addition to the savings and investments that they created to supply them with income during retirement, which includes a traditional IRA, they have also saved money for the sole purpose of purchasing a boat once they stop working.*
>
> *When the time comes and they finally buy the boat of their dreams, they pay an additional $15,000 in sales taxes that year because of the large purchase. Because they are retired and earning less money, the deductions they used to be able to realize from their income taxes are no longer there. The high amount of sales taxes they paid on the boat puts them in a*

position where they could benefit from taking taxable income from a traditional IRA.

When Darrel and Linda's financial professional learns about their purchase, he immediately contacts a CPA at his firm to run the numbers. They determine that by taking a $15,000 distribution from their IRA, they could fulfill their income needs to offset the $15,000 sales tax deduction that they were claiming due to the purchase of their boat. In the end, they pay zero taxes on their income distribution from their IRA.

The moral of the story? ***Having a tax diversified landscape gives you options.*** Having capital assets that can be liquidated, tax-advantaged income options and sources that can create capital gains or capital losses will put you in a position to play your cards right no matter what you want to accomplish with your taxes. The ace up your sleeve is your financial professional and the CPAs they work with. Do yourself a favor and *plan* your taxes instead of *reporting* them!

CHAPTER 11 RECAP //

- You make more money by saving on taxes than you do by making more money. This simple concept becomes extremely valuable to people in retirement and those living on fixed incomes.
- When you pay someone to report your taxes, you are paying to record history. When you *plan* your taxes with a financial professional, you are proactively finding the best options for your tax return.
- The future of U.S. taxation is uncertain. You know what the tax rate and landscape is today, but you won't tomorrow. The only thing you can really count on is the trend of increasing taxation.
- Look for the "free bridge" option in your tax strategy.
- Converting from a traditional to a Roth IRA can provide you with tax-advantaged retirement income.
- Converting to a Roth IRA can also help you preserve and build your legacy.
- There are many ways to reduce your taxes. Being smart about your Roth IRA conversion is one of the main ways to do so.

12

YOUR LEGACY BEYOND DOLLARS AND CENTS

If you're like most people, planning your estate isn't on the top of your list of things to do. Planning your income needs for retirement, managing your assets and just living your life without worrying about how your estate will be handled when you are gone makes legacy planning less than attractive for a Saturday afternoon task. The fact of the matter, however, is that if you don't plan your legacy, someone else will. That someone else is usually a combination of the IRS and other government entities: lawyers, executors, courts, and accountants. Who do you think has the best interests of your beneficiaries in mind?

Today, there is more consideration given to planning a legacy than just maximizing your estate. When most people think about an estate, it may seem like something only the very wealthy have: a stately manor or an enormous business. But a legacy is something else entirely. A legacy is more than the sum total of the financial assets you have accumulated. It is the lasting impression you make on those you leave behind. The dollar and cents are just a small part of a legacy.

A legacy encompasses the stories that others tell about you, shared experiences and values. An estate may pay for college tuition, but a legacy may inform your grandchildren about the importance of higher education and self-reliance.

A legacy may also contain family heirlooms or items of emotional significance. It may be a piece of art your great-grandmother painted, family photos, or a childhood keepsake.

When you go about planning your legacy, certainly explore strategies that can maximize the financial benefit to the ones you care about. But also take the time to ensure that you have organized the whole of your legacy, and let that be a part of a last gift you leave for others.

Many people avoid planning their legacy until they feel they must. Something may change in your life, like the birth of a grandchild, the diagnosis of a serious health problem, or the death of a close friend or loved one. Waiting for tragedy to strike in order to get your affairs in order is not the best course of action. The emotional stress of that kind of situation can make it hard to make patient, thoughtful decisions. Taking the time to create a premeditated and thoughtful legacy plan will assure that your assets will be transferred where and when you want them when the time comes.

THE BENEFITS OF PLANNING YOUR LEGACY

The distribution of your assets, whether in the form of property, stocks, Individual Retirement Accounts, 401(k)s or liquid assets, can be a complicated process if you haven't left clear instructions about how you want them handled. Not having a plan will cost more money and take more time, leaving your loved ones to wait (sometimes for years) and receive less of your legacy than if you had a clear plan.

Planning your legacy will help your assets be transferred with little delay and little confusion. Instead of leaving decisions about how to distribute your estate to your family, attorneys or financial professionals, preserve your legacy and your wishes by drafting a clear plan at an early age.

And while you know all that, it can still be hard to sit down and do it. It reminds you that life is short, and the relatively complicated nature of sorting through your assets can feel like a daunting task. But one thing is for sure: *it is impossible for your assets to be transferred or distributed the way you want at the end of your life if you don't have a plan.*

Ask yourself:

- Are my assets up to date?
- Have my primary and contingent beneficiaries been clearly designated?
- Does my plan allow for restriction of a beneficiary?
- Does my legacy plan address minor children that I want to provide with income?
- Does my legacy plan allow for multi-generational payout to my children and grandchildren?

Answers to these questions are critical if you want the final say in how your assets are distributed. In order to achieve your legacy goals, you need a plan.

MAKING A PLAN

Eventually, when your income need is filled and you have sufficient standby money to meet your need for emergencies, travel or other extra expenses you are planning for, whatever isn't used during your lifetime becomes your financial legacy. The money that you do not use during your lifetime will either go to loved ones, unloved ones, charity, or the IRS. The question is, who would you rather disinherit?

By having a legacy plan that clearly outlines your assets, your beneficiaries and your distribution goals, you can make sure that your money and property is ending up in the hands of the people you determine beforehand. Is it really that big of a deal? It absolutely is. Think about it. Without a clear plan, it is impossible for anyone to know if your beneficiary designations are current and reflect your wishes because you haven't clearly expressed who your beneficiaries are. You may have an idea of who you want your assets to go to, but without a plan, it is anyone's guess. It is also impossible to know if the titling of your assets is accurate unless you have gone through and determined whose name is on the titles. More importantly, *if you have not clearly and effectively communicated your desires regarding the planned distribution of your legacy, you and your family may end up losing a large part of it.*

As you can see, managing a legacy is more complicated than having an attorney read your will, divide your estate and write checks to your heirs. The additional issue of taxes, Family Maximum Benefit calculations and a host of other decisions rear their heads. Educating yourself about the best options for positioning your legacy assets is a challenging undertaking. Working with a financial professional who is versed in determining the most efficient and effective ways of preserving and distributing your legacy can save you time, money and strife.

So, how do you begin?

Making a Legacy Plan Starts with a Simple List. The first, and one of the largest, steps to setting up an estate plan with a financial professional that reflects your desires is creating a detailed inventory of your assets and debts (if you have any). You need to know what assets you have, who the beneficiaries are, how much they are worth and how they are titled. You can start by identifying and listing your assets. This is a good starting point for working with a financial professional who can then help you determine the detailed information about your assets that will dictate how they are distributed upon your death.

If you are particularly concerned about leaving your kids and grandkids a lifetime of income with minimal taxes, you will want to discuss a Stretch IRA option with your financial professional.

THE IMPORTANCE OF A GOOD ESTATE AND FINANCIAL PLAN

Estate planning for the less than wealthy

Most people do not pay estate taxes, but some people still ruin their estate plan. When was the last time your attorney reviewed your will or trust? Did you think it would be good forever in the face of laws that Congress loves to change? What about the other documents? If you're not sure what other documents should be included, ask yourself three questions:

1. Who will take care of my finances if I become incapacitated due to an injury or illness? A durable power of attorney is a method to arrange for someone to do this for you. It can take effect immediately or it can be written with a springing power, meaning that it will not be in force until a certain action takes place. You can specify the action, such as a doctor, or even two, declaring you are unable to make financial decisions. You can stipulate how much control your attorney-in-fact will have over your finances. These powers can include but are not limited to:

- paying household expenses
- handling retirement accounts
- collecting government benefits
- filing income tax returns
- managing a business

- buying and selling assets
- making gifts

The person you select to be your attorney-in-fact should be someone you trust and who has shown the ability to manage his or her own finances competently. This could be a family member, close friend, or your attorney or accountant. You should also consider naming an alternate just in case your first selection is unable or unwilling to carry out the tasks when needed.

2. What will happen if I can no longer make medical decisions for myself? A medical power of attorney, also known as a "health care proxy", a "durable power of attorney for health care," or a "medical directive," gives someone else the legal authority to make medical decisions for you when you can no longer make them for yourself. An alternate should also be named.

3. Under what circumstances would I want medical support to stop? A living will provides specific instructions to your family and physician regarding continuation of your life by artificial means or "heroic measures." This document can relieve your loved ones of the responsibility of making a difficult choice. A living trust can give instructions in case of a remarriage, special needs, or other living situation that needs legal instructions.

HOW MUCH LONG TERM CARE INSURANCE DO I NEED?

When it comes to any type of insurance, you should consider how much risk you can afford to take on your own and how much you want to pass off to the insurance company. The more you are willing to pay out of pocket, the lower the insurance premiums. Pretty simple concept, except in the case of long term care.

The problem with planning for long term care is that you don't know how incapacitated you're going to be and for how long you'll need the care. Every case is different. Therefore, you should do an analysis of your financial and personal situation that includes the cost of long term care in your state, your life expectancy and what tradeoffs you are willing to make.

Let's assume that you and your spouse have $20,000 coming in from Social Security benefits and $30,000 from a pension on an annual basis. This combined income of $50,000 covers all of your expenses. You also have savings and investments totaling $300,000 that has averaged a seven percent return over the past five years. The average annual cost of a nursing home stay is $50,000. If either you or your spouse needed this care, where would the money come from? Whoever is still at home could cut back on his or her expenses, but that rarely helps since the one in the nursing home may need additional medications and incidentals not covered by health insurance.

You could withdraw $21,000 (seven percent) from your investments and not touch the principal, but you would still be $34,000 short. If you take out the full $50,000 needed, your portfolio would be gone in less than seven years.

In the above example, one way to make up the $34,000 shortage would be to purchase a long term care policy that pays $95.00 per day. Another would be to buy a less expensive policy with a lower daily benefit. This means taking on a greater portion of the costs yourself and using some of the portfolio's principal. Either alternative could work. It comes down to your comfort level to assume more of the risks.

If you are uninsurable or do not want to purchase long term care insurance, a retirement planning expert can recommend other options. You have to do something to prepare for the future, and a professional can help you consider all of your options.

STRETCH IRAS: GETTING THE MOST OUT OF YOUR MONEY

In 1986, the U.S. Congress passed a law that allows for multi-generational distributions of IRA assets. This type of distribution is called a Stretch IRA because it stretches the distribution of the account out over a longer period of time to several beneficiaries. It also allows the account to continue accumulating value throughout the lifetime of your relatives. You can use a Stretch IRA as an income tool that distributes throughout your lifetime, your children's lifetimes and your grandchildren's lifetimes.

A stretch IRA is simply a wealth transfer vehicle that gives you the option to "stretch" the value of your IRA across future generations. When an IRA account holder dies, the account often can directly pass to a spouse or other family member by beneficiary designation or by contract. The potential disadvantage of this is the fact that it could force the person who inherits the account into a higher tax bracket. "Stretching" your IRA by naming younger beneficiaries like children or grandchildren can prolong the distribution phase of the IRA and potentially help your loved ones avoid being subjected to the higher taxes to which their IRA inheritance could expose them.

Stretch IRAs are an attractive option for those more concerned with creating income for their loved ones rather than leaving them with a lump sum that may be subject to a high tax rate. With traditional IRA distributions, non-spousal beneficiaries must generally take distributions from their inherited IRAs, whether transferred or not, within five years after the death of the IRA owner. An exception to this rule applies if the beneficiary elects to take distributions over his or her lifetime, which is referred to as stretching the IRA.

Let's begin by looking at the potential of stretching an IRA throughout multiple generations.

» In this scenario, Mr. Cleaver has an IRA with a current balance of $350,000. If we assume a five percent annual rate of return, and a 28 percent tax rate, the Stretch IRA turned a $502,625 legacy into more than $1.5 million. Doubling the value of the IRA also provided Mr. Cleaver, his wife, two children and three grandchildren with income. Not choosing the stretch option would have cost nearly $800,000 and had impacts on six of Mr. Cleaver's loved ones.

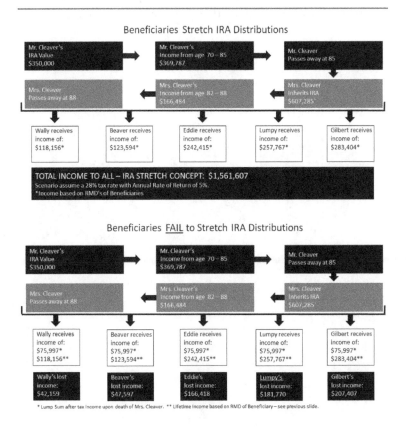

Beneficiaries Stretch IRA Distributions

| Mr. Cleaver's IRA Value $350,000 | Mr. Cleaver's Income from age 70 – 85 $369,787 | Mr. Cleaver Passes away at 85 |
| Mrs. Cleaver Passes away at 88 | Mrs. Cleaver's Income from age 82 – 88 $166,484 | Mrs. Cleaver Inherits IRA $607,285* |

| Wally receives income of: $118,156* | Beaver receives income of: $123,594* | Eddie receives income of: $242,415* | Lumpy receives income of: $257,767* | Gilbert receives income of: $283,404* |

TOTAL INCOME TO ALL – IRA STRETCH CONCEPT: $1,561,607
Scenario assume a 28% tax rate with Annual Rate of Return of 5%.
*Income based on RMD's of Beneficiaries

Beneficiaries **FAIL** to Stretch IRA Distributions

| Mr. Cleaver's IRA Value $350,000 | Mr. Cleaver's Income from age 70 – 85 $369,787 | Mr. Cleaver Passes away at 85 |
| Mrs. Cleaver Passes away at 88 | Mrs. Cleaver's Income from age 82 – 88 $166,484 | Mrs. Cleaver Inherits IRA $607,285* |

| Wally receives income of: $75,997* $118,156** | Beaver receives income of: $75,997* $123,594** | Eddie receives income of: $75,997* $242,415** | Lumpy receives income of: $75,997* $257,767** | Gilbert receives income of: $75,997* $283,404** |

| Wally's lost income: $42,159 | Beaver's lost income: $47,597 | Eddie's lost income: $166,418 | Lumpy's lost income: $181,770 | Gilbert's lost income: $207,407 |

* Lump Sum after tax income upon death of Mrs. Cleaver. ** Lifetime income based on RMD of Beneficiary – see previous slide.

Unfortunately, many things may also play a role in failing to stretch IRA distributions. It can be tempting for a beneficiary to take a lump sum of money despite the tax consequences. Fortunately, if you want to solidify your plan for distribution, there are options that will allow you to open up an IRA and incorporate "spendthrift" clauses for your beneficiaries. This will ensure your legacy is stretched appropriately and to your specifications. Only certain insurance companies allow this option and you will not find this benefit with any brokerage accounts. You need to work with a financial professional who has the appropriate relationship with an insurance company that provides this option.

13

PREPARING YOUR LEGACY

David organized his assets long ago. He started planning his retirement early and made investment decisions that would meet his needs. With a combination of IRA to Roth IRA conversions, a series of income annuities and a well-planned money management strategy overseen by his financial professional, he easily filled his income gap and was able to focus on ways to accumulate his wealth throughout his retirement. He reorganized his Protected and Unprotected Money as he got older. When David retired, he had an income plan created that allowed him to maximize his Social Security benefit. He even had enough to accumulate wealth during his retirement. At this point, David turned his attention to planning his legacy. He wanted to know how he could maximize the amount of the legacy he will pass on to his heirs.

David met with an attorney to draw up a will and quickly learned that while having a will was a good plan, it wasn't the most efficient way to distribute his legacy. In fact, relying solely on a will created several roadblocks.

The two main problems that arose for David were *Probate* and *Unintentional Disinheritance:*

Problem #1: Probate

Probate. Just speaking the word out loud can cause shivers to run down your spine. Probate's ugly reputation is well deserved. It can be a costly, time consuming process that diminishes your estate and can delay the distribution of your estate to your loved ones. It's nasty stuff by any measure. Unless you have made a clear legacy plan and discussed options for avoiding probate, it is highly likely that you have many assets that might pass through probate needlessly. ***If your will and beneficiary designations aren't correctly structured, some of these assets will go through the probate process, which can turn dollars into cents.***

If you have a will, probate is usually just a formality. There is little risk that your will won't be executed per your instructions. The problem arises when the costs and lengthy timeline that probate creates come into play. Probate proceedings are notoriously expensive, lengthy and ponderous. A typical probate process identifies all of your assets and debts, pays any taxes and fees that you owe (including estate tax), pays court fees, and distributes your property and assets to your heirs. This process usually takes at least a year, and can take even longer before your heirs actually receive anything that you have left for them. For this reason, and because of the sometimes exorbitant fees that may be charged by lawyers and accountants during the process, probate has earned a nasty reputation.

Probate can also be a painstakingly public process. Because the probate process happens in court, the assets you own that go through a probate procedure become part of the public record. While this may not seem like a big deal to some, other people don't want that kind of intimate information available to the public.

Additionally, if your estate is entirely distributed via your will, the money that your family may need to cover the costs of your medical bills, funeral expenses and estate taxes will be tied up in probate, which can last up to a year or more. While immediate family members may have the option of requesting immediate cash from your assets during probate to cover immediate health care expenses, taxes, and fees, that process comes with its own set of complications. Choosing alternative methods for distributing your legacy can make life easier for your loved ones and can help them claim more of your estate in a more timely fashion than traditional methods.

A simpler and less tedious approach is to avoid probate altogether by structuring your estate to be distributed outside of the probate process. Two common ways of doing this are by structuring your assets inside a life insurance plan, and by using individual retirement planning tools like IRAs that give you the option of designating a beneficiary upon your death.

Problem #2: Unintentionally Disinheriting Your Family

You would never want to unintentionally disinherit a loved one or loved ones because of confusion surrounding your legacy plan. Unfortunately, it happens. Why? This terrible situation is typically caused by a simple lack of understanding. In particular, mistakes regarding legacy distribution occur with regard to those whom people care for the most: their grandchildren.

One of the most important ways to plan for the inheritance of your grandchildren is by properly structuring the distribution of your legacy. Specifically, you need to know if your legacy is going to be distributed *per stirpes* or *per capita*.

Per Stirpes. *Per stirpes* is a legal term in Latin that means "by the branch." Your estate will be distributed *per stirpes* if you designate each branch of your family to receive an equal share of your estate. In the event that your children predecease you, their share will be distributed evenly between their children—your grandchildren.

Per Capita. *Per capita* distribution is different in that you may designate different amounts of your estate to be distributed to members of the same generation.

Per stirpes distribution of assets will follow the family tree down the line as the predecessor beneficiaries pass away. On the other hand, per capita distribution of assets ends on the branch of the family tree with the death of a designated beneficiary. For example, when your child passes away, in a per capita distribution, your grandchildren would not receive distributions from the assets that you designated to your child.

What the terms mean is not nearly as important as what they do, however. The reality is that improperly titled assets could accidentally leave your grandchildren disinherited upon the death of their parents. It's easy to check, and it's even easier to fix.

Another way to avoid complicated legacy distribution problems, and the probate process, is by leveraging a life insurance plan.

LIFE INSURANCE: AN IMPORTANT LEGACY TOOL

One of the most powerful legacy tools you can leverage is a good life insurance policy. Life insurance is a highly efficient legacy tool because it creates money when it is needed or desired the most. Over the years, life insurance has become less expensive, while it offers more features and provides longer guarantees.

There are many unique benefits of life insurance that can help your beneficiaries get the most out of your legacy. Some of them include:

- Providing beneficiaries with a tax-free, liquid asset.

- Covering the costs associated with your death.
- Providing income for your dependents.
- Offering an investment opportunity for your beneficiaries.
- Covering expenses such as tuition or mortgage down payments for your children or grandchildren.

Very few people want life insurance, but nearly everyone wants what it does. Life insurance is specifically, and uniquely, capable of creating money when it is needed most. When a loved one passes, no amount of money can remove the pain of loss. And certainly, money doesn't solve the challenges that might arise with losing someone important.

It has been said that when you have money, you have options. When you don't have money, your options are severely limited. You might imagine a life insurance policy can give your family and loved ones options that would otherwise be impossible.

> » Ben spent the last 20 years building a small business. In so many ways, it is a family business. Each of his three children, Maddie, Ruby and Edward, worked in the shop part-time during high school. But after all three attended college, only Maddie returned to join her father, and eventually will run the business full-time when Ben retires.
>
> Ben is able to retire comfortably on Social Security and on-going income from the shop, but the business is nearly his entire financial legacy. It is his wish that Maddie own the business outright, but he also wants to leave an equal legacy to each of his three children.
>
> There is no simple way to divide the business into thirds and still leave the business intact for Maddie.
>
> Ben ends up buying a life insurance policy to make up the difference. Ruby and Edward will receive their share of an

inheritance in cash from the life insurance policy and Maddie will be able to inherit the business intact.

Ben is able to accomplish his goals, treat all three children equitably and leave Maddie the business she helped to build.

If you have a life insurance policy but you haven't looked at it in a while, you may not know how it operates, how much it is worth and how it will be distributed to your beneficiaries. You may also need to update your beneficiaries on your policy. In short, without a comprehensive review of your policy, you don't really know where the money will go or to whom it will go.

If you don't have a life insurance policy but are looking for options to maintain and grow your legacy, speaking with a professional can show you the benefits of life insurance. Many people don't consider buying a life insurance policy until some event in their life triggers it, like the loss of a loved one, an accident or a health condition.

BENEFITS OF LIFE INSURANCE

Life insurance is a useful and secure tool for contingency planning, ensuring that your dependents receive the assets that you want them to have, and for meeting the financial goals you have set for the future. While it bears the name "Life Insurance," it is, in reality, a diverse financial tool that can meet many needs. The main function of a life insurance policy is to provide financial assets for your survivors. Life insurance is particularly efficient at achieving this goal because it provides a tax-advantaged lump sum of money in the form of a death benefit to your beneficiary or beneficiaries. That financial asset can be used in a number of ways. It can be structured as an investment to provide income for your spouse or children, it can pay down debts, and it can be used to cover estate taxes and other costs associated with death.

Tax liabilities on the estate you leave behind are inevitable. Capital property, for instance, is taxed at its fair market value at the time of your death, unless that property is transferred to your spouse. If the property has appreciated during the time you owned it, taxation on capital gains will occur. Registered Retirement Savings Plans (RRSPs) and other similarly structured assets are also included as taxable income unless transferred to a beneficiary as well. Those are just a few examples of how an estate can become subject to a heavy tax burden. The unique benefits of a life insurance policy provide ways to handle this tax burden, solving any liquidity problems that may arise if your family members want to hold onto an illiquid asset, such as a piece of property or an investment. Life insurance can provide a significant amount of money to a family member or other beneficiary. That money is likely to remain exempt from taxation or seizure.

One of life insurance's most important benefits is that it is not considered part of the estate of the policy holder. The death benefit that is paid by the insurance company goes exclusively to the beneficiaries listed on the policy. This shields the proceeds of the policy from fees and costs that can reduce an estate, including probate proceedings, attorneys' fees and claims made by creditors. The distribution of your life insurance policy is also unaffected by delays of the estate's distribution, like probate. Your beneficiaries will get the proceeds of the policy in a timely fashion, regardless of how long it takes for the rest of your estate to be settled.

Investing a portion of your assets in a life insurance policy can also protect that portion of your estate from creditors. If you owe money to someone or some entity at the time of your death, a creditor is not able to claim any money from a life insurance policy or an annuity, unless you had already used the life insurance policy as collateral against a loan. If a large portion of the money you want to dedicate to your legacy is sitting in a savings account, investment or other liquid form, creditors may be able to receive their claim on it before your beneficiaries get anything; that is, if there's anything left. A life insurance policy protects your assets from creditors and ensures that your beneficiaries get the money that you intend them to have.

HOW MUCH LIFE INSURANCE DO YOU NEED?

Determining the type of policy and the amount right for you depends on an analysis of your needs. A financial professional can help you complete a needs analysis that will highlight the amount of insurance that you require to meet your goals. This type of personalized review will allow you to determine ways to continue providing income for your spouse or any dependents you may have. A financial professional can also help you calculate the amount of income that your policy should replace to meet the needs of your beneficiaries and the duration of the distribution of that income.

You may also want to use your life insurance policy to meet any expenses associated with your death. These can include funeral costs, fees from probate, legal proceedings and taxes. You may also want to dedicate a portion of your policy proceeds to help fund tuition or other expenses for your children or grandchildren. You can buy a policy and hope it covers all of those costs, or you can work with a professional who can calculate exactly how much insurance you need and how to structure it to meet your goals. Which would you rather do?

AVOIDING POTENTIAL SNAGS

There are benefits to having life insurance supersede the direction given in a will or other estate plan, but there are also some potential snags that you should address to meet your wishes. For example, if your will instructs that your assets be divided equally between your two children but your life insurance beneficiary is listed as just one of the children, the assets in the life insurance policy will only be distributed to the child listed as the beneficiary. The beneficiary designation of your life insurance supersedes your will's instruction. This is important to understand when designating beneficiaries on a policy you purchase. Work with a professional to make sure that your beneficiaries are accurately listed on your assets, especially your life insurance policies.

USING LIFE INSURANCE TO BUILD YOUR LEGACY

Depending on your goals, there are strategies you can use that could multiply how much you leave behind. Life insurance is one of the most surefire and efficient investment tools for building a substantial legacy that will meet your financial goals.

Here is a brief overview of how life insurance can boost your legacy:

- Life insurance provides an immediate increase in your legacy.
- It provides an income tax-advantaged death benefit for your beneficiaries.
- A good life insurance policy has the opportunity to accumulate value over time.
- It may have an option to include long-term care (LTC) or chronic illness benefits should you require them.

If your Green Money income needs for retirement are met and you have Yellow Money assets that will provide for your future expenses, you may have extra assets that you want to earmark as legacy funds. By electing to invest those assets into a life insurance policy, you can immediately increase the amount of your legacy. Remember, **life insurance allows you to transfer a tax-advantaged lump sum of money to your beneficiaries. It remains in your control during your lifetime, can provide for your long-term care needs and bypasses probate costs.** And make no mistake; taxes can have a huge impact on your legacy.

Not only that, income and assets from your legacy can have tax implications for your beneficiaries, as well.

Here's a brief overview of how taxes could affect your legacy and your beneficiaries:

- The higher your income, the higher the rate at which it is taxed.
- Withdrawals from qualified plans are taxed as income.
- What's more, when you leave a large qualified plan, it ends up being taxed at a high rate.
- If you left a $500,000 IRA to your child, they could end up owing as much as $140,000 in income taxes.
- However, if you could just withdraw $50,000 a year, the tax bill might only be $10,000 per year.

How could you use that annual amount to leave a larger legacy? Luckily, you can leverage a life insurance policy to avoid those tax penalties, preserving a larger amount of your legacy and freeing your beneficiaries from an added tax burden.

> » *When Brenda turned 70 years old, she decided it was time to look into life insurance policy options. She still feels young, but she remembers that her mother died in early 70s, and she wants to plan ahead so she can pass on some of her legacy to her grandchildren just like her grandmother did for her.*
>
> *Brenda doesn't really want to think about life insurance, but she does want the security, reliability and tax-advantaged distribution that it offers. She lives modestly, and her Social Security benefit meets most of her income needs. As the beneficiary of her late husband's Certificate of Deposit (CD), she has $100,000 in an account that she has never used and doesn't anticipate ever needing since her income needs were already met.*

*After looking at several different investment options with a professional, Brenda decides that a Single Premium life insurance policy fits her needs best. She can buy the policy with a $100,000 one-time payment and she is guaranteed that it would provide more than the value of the contract to her beneficiaries. If she left the money in the CD, it would be subject to taxes. For every dollar she puts into the life insurance policy, her beneficiaries are guaranteed at least that dollar plus a death benefit, and all of it will be **tax-free!***

For $100,000, Brenda's particular policy offers a $170,000 death benefit distribution to her beneficiaries. By moving the $100,000 from a CD to a life insurance policy, Brenda increases her legacy by 70 percent. Not only that, she has also sheltered it from taxes, so her beneficiaries will be able to receive $1.70 for every $1.00 that she put into the policy! While buying the policy doesn't allow her to use the money for herself, it does allow her family to benefit from her well-planned legacy.

MAKE YOUR WISHES KNOWN

Estate taxes used to be a much hotter topic in the mid-2000s when the estate tax limits and exclusions were much smaller and taxed at a higher rate than today. In 2008, estates valued at $2 million or more were taxed at 45 percent. Just two years later, the limit was raised to $5 million dollars taxed at 35 percent. The limit has continued to rise ever since. The limit applies to fewer people than before. Estate organization, however, is just as important as ever and it affects everyone.

Ask yourself:

- Are your assets actually titled and held the way you think they are?
- Are your beneficiaries set up the way you think they should be?

- Have there been changes to your family or those you desire as beneficiaries?

There is more to your legacy beyond your property, money, investments and other assets that you leave to family members, loved ones and charities. Everyone has a legacy beyond money. You also leave behind personal items of importance, your values and beliefs, your personal and family history and your wishes. Besides having a will and a plan for your assets, it is important that you make your wishes known to someone for the rest of your personal legacy. When it comes time for your family and loved ones to make decisions after you are gone, knowing your wishes can help them make decisions that honor you and your legacy and give meaning to what you leave behind. Your professional can help you organize.

Think about your:
- Personal stories/recollections
- Values
- Personal items of emotional significance
- Financial assets

Do you want to make a plan to pass these things on to your family?

WORKING WITH A PROFESSIONAL

Part of using life insurance to your greatest advantage is selecting the policy and provider that can best meet your goals. Venturing into the jungle of policies, brokers and salespeople can be overwhelming and can leave you wondering if you've made the best decision. Working with a trusted financial professional can help you cut through the red tape, the "sales-speak" and confusion to find a policy that meets your goals and best serves your desires for your money. If you already have a policy, a financial professional can help you review it and become familiar with the policy's premium, the guarantees the policy affords, its performance, features and benefits. A financial professional can also help you make any necessary changes to the policy.

> » *When Cheryl turned 88, her daughter finally convinced her to meet with a financial professional to help her organize her assets and get her legacy in order. Although Cheryl is reluctant to let a stranger in on her personal finances, she ends up very glad that she did.*
>
> *In the process of listing Cheryl's assets and her beneficiaries, her professional finds a man's name listed as the beneficiary of an old life insurance annuity that she owns. It turns out, the man is Cheryl's ex-husband who is still alive. Had Cheryl passed away before her ex-husband, the annuities and any death benefits that came with them, would have been passed on to her ex-husband. This does not reflect her latest wishes.*

Things change, relationships evolve and the way you would like your legacy organized needs to adapt to the changes that happen throughout your life. There may be a new child or grandchild in your family, or you may have been divorced or remarried. A professional will regularly review your legacy assets and ask you questions to make sure that everything is up to date and that the current organization reflects your current wishes.

CHAPTER 13 RECAP //

- You can structure your assets in ways that maximize distributions to your beneficiaries.

- Working with a financial professional can help ensure that many of your assets avoid the ponderous and expensive probate process.

- A financial professional can help review the details of the assets you have designated to be a part of your legacy and make sure that you aren't unintentionally disinheriting your heirs.

- Life insurance provides the distribution of tax-free, liquid assets to your beneficiaries.

- Investing in a life insurance policy can significantly build your legacy.

- Organizing your estate will allow you to make sure your wishes are properly carried through.

- You can take advantage of a "Stretch IRA" to provide income for you, your spouse and your beneficiaries throughout their lifetimes.

- Understand if your assets will be distributed *per stirpes* or *per capita*.

- Working with a financial professional can help you select the policy that best meets your needs, or can help you fine tune your existing policy to better reflect your desires and intentions.

- Your professional should make an up-to-date list of all your tangible assets and how to access each of them. This list should be updated periodically.

14

CHOOSING A FINANCIAL PROFESSIONAL

From the moment you dip your toes into the retirement planning pool to the point you start swimming laps, your assets organized, your income needs met, and your accumulation and legacy plans in place, working with a professional that you trust can make all the difference in how well your retirement reflects your desires.

It is important to know what you are looking for before taking the plunge. There are many people that would love to handle your money, but not everyone is qualified to handle it in a way that leads to a holistic approach to creating a solid retirement plan.

The distinction being made here is that you should look for someone that puts your interests first and actively wants to help you meet your goals and objectives. A comprehensive plan that meets your needs is a better approach to retirement than any one product.

Professionals take your whole financial position into consideration. They make plans that adjust your risk exposure, invest in tools that secure your desired income during retirement and create investment strategies that allow you to continue accumulating wealth during your retirement for you to use later or to contribute to your legacy. If you buy stocks with a broker, use a different agent for a life insurance policy and have an unmanaged 401(k) through your employer, working with a financial professional will consolidate the management of your assets so you have one trustworthy person quarterbacking all of the team elements of your portfolio. Financial products and investment tools change, but the concepts that lie behind wise retirement planning are lasting. In the end, a financial professional's approach is designed for those serious about planning for retirement. *Can you say the same thing about the person that advises you about your financial life?*

It's easy to see how choosing a financial professional can be one of the most important decisions you can make in your life. Not only do they provide you with advice, they also manage the personal assets that supply your retirement income and contribute to your legacy. So, how do you find a good one?

HOW TO FIND A FINANCIAL PROFESSIONAL YOU CAN TRUST

Taking care to select a financial professional is one of the best things you can do for yourself and for your future. Your professional has influence and control of your investment decisions, making their role in your life more than just important. Your financial security and the quality of your retirement depend on the decisions, investment strategies and asset structuring that you and your professional create.

Working with a professional is different from calling up a broker when you want to buy or trade some stock. This isn't a decision that you can hand off to anyone else. You need to bring your time and attention to the table when it comes to finding someone with whom you can entrust your financial life. Separating the wheat from the chaff will take some work, but you'll be happy you did it.

While no one can tell you exactly who to choose or how to choose them, the following information can help you narrow the field:

- You can start by asking your friends, family and colleagues for referrals. You will want to pay particular attention to the recommendations that you get from others who are in your similar financial situation and who have similar lifestyle choices. The professional for the CEO of your company may have a different skill-set than the skill-set of the professional befitting your cousin who has 3 kids and a Subaru like you. Do follow-up research on the Internet as well. Look up the people who have been recommended to you on websites like LinkedIn that show the work history, referrals and experience of the candidates that you find most attractive. You will also learn about the firms with or for whom they work. The investment philosophies and reputations of the companies they work for will tell you a lot about how they will handle your money.

- The other side of the coin, however, is that everyone and their brother has a recommendation about how you should manage your money and who should manage it for you. From hot stock tips to "the best money manager in the state," people love to share good information that makes them look like they are in-the-know. Nobody wants to talk about the bad stock purchases they made, the times they lost money and the poor selections they made regarding financial professionals or stock brokers. If you decide to take a friend or family member's recommendation, make sure they have a substantial, long-term experience with the financial professional and that their glowing review isn't just based on a one-time "win."

- You can also use online tools like the search function of the Financial Planning Association (http://www.fpanet. org/) and the National Association of Personal Financial Advisors (http://www.napfa.org/). Most of the professionals listed on these sites do not earn commissions from selling financial products, but are instead paid on a fee-only basis for their services. It is important to understand how your professional is being paid. It is generally considered preferable to work with a fee-based professional who will not have conflicts of interests between earning a commission and acting in your best interests.

- Many professionals may also be brokers or dealers that can earn commissions on things like life insurance, certain types of annuities and disability insurance. These professionals have most likely intentionally overlapped their roles so that if their clients choose to purchase insurance or investment products that require a broker or dealer, those clients won't have to find an additional person to work with. Again, understanding the role of your professional will help you make your determination.

NARROWING THE FIELD

1. Decide on the Type of Professional with Whom You Want to Work. There are four basic kinds of financial professionals. Many professionals may play overlapping roles. It is important to know a professional's primary function, how they charge for their services and whether they are obligated to act in your best interest.

Registered representatives, better known as stockbrokers or bank / investment representatives, make their living by earning commissions on insurance products and investment services. Stockbrokers basically sell you things. The products from which they make the highest commission are sometimes the products that they recommend to their clients. If you want to make a simple transaction, such as buying or selling a particular stock, a registered representative can help you. Although registered representatives are licensed professionals, if you want to create a structured and planful approach to positioning your assets for retirement, you might want to consider continuing your search.

The term "planner" is often misused. It can refer to credible professionals that are CPAs, CFPs and ChFCs to your uncle's next door neighbor who claims to have a lead on some undervalued stock about to be "discovered." A wide array of people may claim to be planners because there are no requirements to be a planner. The term financial planner, however, refers to someone who is properly registered as an investment advisor and serves as a fiduciary as described below.

Financial professionals are the diamonds in the rough. These Registered Investment Advisors are compensated on a fee basis. They do, however, often have licensure as stockbrokers or insurance agents, allowing them to earn commissions on certain transactions. More importantly, **financial professionals are financial fiduciaries, meaning they are required to make financial decisions in your best interest and reflecting your risk tolerance.** Investment Advisors are held to high ethical standards and are highly regarded in the financial industry. Financial professionals also often take a more comprehensive approach to asset management. These professionals are trained and credentialed to plan and coordinate their clients' assets in order to meet their goals or retirement and legacy planning. They are not focused on individual stocks, investments or markets. They look at the big picture, the whole enchilada.

Money managers are on par with financial professionals. However, they are often given explicit permission to make investment decisions without advanced approval by their clients.

Understanding who you are working with and what their title is the first step to planning your retirement. While each of the above-mentioned types of financial professionals can help you with aspects of your finances, it is financial professionals who have the most intimate role, the most objective investment strategies and the most unbiased mode of compensation for their services. A financial professional can also help you with the non-financial aspects of your legacy and can help you find ways to create a tax planning strategy to help you save money.

2. Be Objective. At the end of the day, you need to separate the weak from the strong. While you might want a strong personal rapport with your professional and might want to choose them for their personality and positive attitude, it is more important that you find someone who will give sage advice regarding achieving your retirement goals.

It can be helpful to use a process of elimination to narrow the field of potential professionals. Look into five or six potential leads and cross off your list the ones that don't meet your requirements until only one or two remain. Cross-check your remaining choices against the list of things you need from a professional. Make sure they represent a firm that has the investment tools and products that you desire, and make sure they have experience in retirement planning. That is, after all, the main goal.

Don't be afraid to investigate each of your candidates. You'll want to ask the same questions and look for the same information from everyone you consider so you can then compare them and discern which is best for you. You'll want to take a look at the specific credentials of each professional, their experience and competence, their ethics and fiduciary status, their history and track record, and a list of the services that they offer. The professionals who meet all or most of your qualifications are the ones you will contact for an interview.

Potential professionals should meet your qualifications in the following categories:

- *Credentials:* Look at their experience, the quality of their education, any associations to which they belong and certifications they have earned. Someone who has continued their professional education through ongoing certifications will be more up-to-date on current financial practices compared to someone who got their degree 25 years ago and hasn't done a thing since.

- *Practices:* Look at the track record of your candidates, how they are compensated for their services, the reports and analysis they offer, and their value added services.

- *Services:* Your professional must meet your needs. If you are planning your retirement, you should work with someone who offers services that help you to that end. You want someone who can offer planning, advice on investment strategies, ways to calculate risk, advice on insurance and annuities products, and ways to manage your tax strategy.

- *Ethics:* You want to work with someone who is above board and does things the right way. Vet them by checking their compliance record, current licensing, fiduciary status and, yes, even their criminal record. You never know!

3. Ask for and Check References. Once you have selected two or three professionals that you want to meet, call or email them and ask for references. Every professional should be able to provide you with at least two or three names. In fact, they will probably be eager to share them with you. Most professionals rely on references for validation of their success, quality of services and likability. You should, however, take them with a grain of salt. You have no way to know whether or not references are a professional's friends or colleagues.

It is worth contacting references, however, to check for inconsistencies. Ask each reference the same set of questions to get the same basic information. How long have they been working with the professional? What kind of services have they used and were they happy with them? What type of financial planning did they use the professional for? Were they versed in the type of financial planning that you needed? You can also ask them direct questions to elicit candid responses. What was the full cost of the expenses that your professional charged you? Do the reports and statements you receive come from the same firm? Questions like these can help you get a sense of how well the reference knows their professional and whether or not they are a quality reference.

A good reference is a bit like icing on the cake. It's nice to have them, but nothing speaks louder than a good track record and quality experience. Remember that a good reference, while nice to hear, is relatively cheap. How many times have you heard someone on the golf course or at work telling you how great their stockbroker is? How many times have you heard about the bad investments or losses they have experienced?

4. Use the Internet. As a final step before picking up the phone and calling your candidates, do some digging to discover if anyone on your list has a history of unlawful or unethical practices, or has been disciplined for any of their professional behavior or decisions. Don't worry, you don't have to hire a private investigator. You can easily find this information on the Financial Industry Regulatory Authority's (FINRA) online BrokerCheck tool: http:// www.finra.org/Investors/ToolsCalculators/BrokerCheck/. You can also review your Investment Advisory Representative's record or a Registered Investment Advisor Firm's record using the SEC's website at: www.adviserinfo@sec.gov.

You should obviously explore the website of a potential professional and the website of the firm that they represent. The Internet allows you to go beyond the online business card of a professional to gain access to information that they don't control. It may all be good information! Or a brief search of the Internet could reveal a sketchy past. The best part is that the Internet allows you to find helpful information in an anonymous fashion.

Start with Google (www.google.com) and search the name of a potential professional and their firm. Keep your eyes trained on third party sources such as articles, blog posts or news stories that mention the professional. You can also check a professional's compliance records online with the Financial Industry Regulatory Authority (FINRA) and the Securities and Exchange Commission (SEC). (See the website references above.) If you want to dig deeper, you can combine search terms like "scams," "lawsuits," "suspensions" and "fraud" with a professional's or firm's name to see what information arises. More likely than not, you won't find anything. But if you do, you'll be glad that you checked.

HOW TO INTERVIEW CANDIDATES

After vetting your candidates and narrowing down a list of professionals that you think might be a good fit for you, it's time to start interviewing.

When you meet in person with a professional, you want to take advantage of your time with them. The presentations and information that they share with you will be important to pay attention to, but you will also want to control some aspects of the interview. After a professional has told you what they want you to hear, it's time to ask your own questions to get the specific information you need to make your decision.

Make sure to prepare a list of questions and an informal agenda so that you can keep track of what you want to ask and what points you want the professional to touch on during the interview. Using the same questions and agenda will also allow you to more easily compare the professionals after you have interviewed them all. Remember that these interviews are just that, *interviews*. You are meeting with several professionals to determine with whom you want to work. Don't agree to anything or sign anything during an interview until after you have made your final decision.

It can also be helpful to put a time limit on your interviews and to meet the professionals at their offices. The time limit will keep things on track and will allow structured time for presentations and questions/discussion. By meeting them at their office, you can get a sense of the work environment, the staff culture and attitude, and how the firm does business. If you are unable to travel to a professional's office and must meet them at your home or office, make sure that your interviews are scheduled with plenty of time between so the professionals don't cross each other's paths.

You can use the following questions during an initial interview to get an understanding of how each professional does business and whether they are a good fit for you:

1. How do you charge for your services? How much do you charge? This information should be easy to find on their website, but if you don't see it, ask. Find out if they charge an initial planning fee, if they charge a percentage for assets under their management and if they make money by selling specific financial products or services. If so, you should follow up by asking how much the service costs. This will give you an idea of how they really make their money and if they have incentive to sell certain products over others. Make sure you understand exactly how you will be charged so there are no surprises down the road if you decide to work with this person.

2. What are your credentials, licenses, and certifications? There are Certified Financial Planners (CFPs), Chartered Financial Consultants (ChFCs), Investment Advisor Representatives, Certified Public Accountants (CPAs) and Personal Financial Specialists (PFSs). Whatever their credentials or titles, you want to be sure that the professional you work with is an expert in the field relevant to your circumstances. If you want someone to manage your money, you will most likely look for an Investment Advisor. Someone that works with an independent firm will likely have a team of CPAs, CFPs and other financial experts upon whom they can draw. If you like the professional you are meeting with and you think they might be a good fit, but they don't have the accounting experience you want them to have, ask about their firm and the resources available to them. If they work closely with CPAs that are experienced in your needs, it could be a good match.

3. What are the financial services that you and your firm provide? The question within the question here is, "Can you help me achieve my goals?" Some people can only provide you with investment advice, and others are tax consultants. You will likely want to work with someone that provides a complete suite of financial planning services and products that touch on retirement planning, insurance options, legacy and estate structuring and tax planning. Whatever services they provide, make sure they meet your needs and anticipated needs.

4. What kinds of clients do you work with the most? A lot of financial professionals work within a niche: retirement planning, risk assessment, life insurance, etc. Finding someone who works with other people that are in the same financial boat as you and who have similar goals can be an important way to make sure they understand your needs. While someone might be a crackerjack annuities cowboy, you might not be interested in that option. Ask follow-up questions that will really help you understand where their expertise lies and whether or not their experience lines up with your needs.

5. May I see a sample of one of your financial plans? You wouldn't buy a car without test driving it, and you should not work with a professional without seeing a sample of how they do business. While there is no formal structure that a financial plan has to follow, the variation between professionals can help you find someone who "speaks your language." One professional may provide you with an in-depth analysis that relies heavily on info graphics and diagrams. Someone else may give you a seven page review of your assets and general recommendations. By seeing a sample plan, you can narrow down who presents information in the way that you desire and in ways that you understand.

6. How do you approach investing? You may be entirely in the dark about how to approach your investments, or you might have some guiding principles. Either way, ask each candidate what their philosophy is. Some will resonate with you and some won't. A good professional who has a realistic approach to investing won't promise you the moon or tell you that they can make you a lot of money. Professionals who are successful at retirement planning and full service financial management will tell you that they will listen to your goals, risk tolerance and comfort level with different types of investment strategies. Working with someone that you trust is critical, and this question in particular can help you find out who you can and who you can't.

7. How do you remain in contact with your clients? Does your prospective professional hold annual, quarterly or monthly meetings? How often do *you* want to meet with your professional? Some people want to check in once a year, go over everything and make sure their ducks are all in a row. If any changes over the previous year or additions to their legacy planning strategy came up, they'll do it on that date. Other people want a monthly update to be more involved in the decision making process and to understand what's happening with their portfolio. You basically need to determine the right degree of involvement for both you and your financial professional. You'll also want to feel out how your professional communicates. Do you prefer phone calls or face-to-face meetings? Do you want your professional to explain things to you in detail or to summarize for you what decisions they've made? Is the professional willing to give you their direct phone number or their email address? More importantly, do you want that information and do you want to be able to contact them in those ways?

8. Are you my main contact, or do you work with a team? This is another way of finding out how involved with you your professional will be and how often they will meet with you. It is also a way to discover how the firm they represent operates and manages their clients. Some professionals will answer their own phone, meet with you regularly and have your home phone number on speed dial. Others will meet with you once a year and have a partner or assistant check in with you every quarter to give you an update. Other companies take a team-based approach whereby clients have a main contact but their portfolio is handled by a team of professionals that represent the firm. One way isn't better than another, but one way will be best for you. Find out how the professional you are interviewing operates before entering into an agreement.

9. How do you provide a unique experience for your clients? This is a polite way of asking, "Why should I work with you?" A professional should have a compelling answer to this question that connects with you. Their answer will likely touch on their investment philosophy, their communication style and expertise. If you hear them describing strengths and philosophies that resonate with you, keep them on your list. Some professionals will tell you that they will make investments with your money that match your values, others will say they will maximize your returns and others will say they will protect your capital while structuring your assets for income. Whatever you're looking for in a professional, you will most likely find it in the answer to that question.

This last question you will want to ask *yourself* after you've met with someone who you are considering hiring:

10. Did they ask questions and show signs that they were interested in working with me? A professional who will structure your assets to reflect your risk tolerance and position you for a comfortable retirement must be a good listener. You will want to pass by a professional who talks non-stop and tells you what to do without listening to what you want them to do. If you felt they listened well, understood your needs and seemed interested and experienced in your situation, they might be right for you.

THE IMPORTANCE OF INDEPENDENCE

Not all investment firms and financial professionals are created equal. The information in this book has systematically shown that leveraging investments for income and accumulation in today's market requires new ideas and modern planning. In short, you need innovative ideas to come up with the creative solutions that will provide you with the retirement that you want. Innovation thrives on independence. No matter how good a financial professional is, the firm that they represent needs to operate on principles that make sense in today's economy. Remember, advice about money has been around forever. Good advice, however, changes with the times.

Timing the market, relying on the sale of stocks for income and banking on high treasury and bond returns are not strategies. They aren't realistic ways to make money or to generate income. Working with an independent agent can help you break free from the old ways of thinking and position you to create a realistic retirement plan.

Working with an independent professional who relies on fee-based income tied to the success of their performance will also give you greater peace of mind. When you do well, they do well, and that's the way it should be. Your independent financial professional will make sure that:

- Your assets are organized and structured to reflect your risk tolerance.
- Your assets will be available to you when you need them and in the way that you need them.
- You will have a lifetime income that will support your lifestyle through your retirement.
- You are handling your taxes as efficiently as possible.
- Your legacy is in order.
- Your Red Money is turned into Yellow Money, and is managed in your best interest.

» *Remember Jack and Beverly from Chapter 1? Even though they knew they had Social Security benefits coming, they placed some money in savings and each had a pension or a 401(k).* **Before they met with a financial professional, they had no idea what their retirement would look like.** *After they met with an agent, they knew exactly what types of assets they had, how much they were worth, how much risk they were exposed to and how they were going to be distributed. They also created an income plan so that they could* *pay their bills every month the moment they retired and they maximized their Social Security benefit by targeting the year and month they would get the most lifetime benefits. After their income needs were met, they were able to continue accumulating wealth by investing their extra assets to serve them in the future and contribute to their legacy. Their professional also helped them make decisions that impacted their taxes, protecting the value of their assets and allowing them to keep more of their money.*

*This isn't a fairy tale scenario. This is an example of how much you stand to gain by meeting with a financial professional who can help you create a planful approach to your retirement. The concept of Protected and Unprotected didn't just apply to their money, it also applied to Jack and Beverly. They **hoped** they would have enough for retirement and that they had worked hard enough and saved enough to maintain their lifestyle. Working with a financial professional allowed them to **know** that their income needs were secured and structured to provide them with income for the rest of their lives with some money to spare.*

Now, ask yourself: Is your retirement built on hopes and dreams, or a solid, predictable plan?

IT'S WORTH IT!

Finding, interviewing and selecting a financial professional can seem like a daunting task. And honestly, it will take a good amount of work to narrow the field and find the one you want. In the end, it's worth the blood, sweat and tears. Your retirement, lifestyle, assets and legacy is on the line. The choices you make today will have lasting impacts on your life and the life of your loved ones. Working with someone you trust and know you can rely on to make decisions that will benefit you is invaluable. The work it takes to find them is something you will never regret.

Here is a recap of why working with a retirement planning expert is the best retirement decision you can make:

CHAPTER 14 RECAP //

- If you feel you have more *Unprotected Money* than *Protected Money,* working with a financial professional will give you clarity and confidence about what decisions are best for you.
- It is difficult for individual investors to not make emotional decisions about their investments. Financial professionals work with your risk tolerance, income needs and assets to find the most logical, efficient and beneficial way for you to structure your investments.
- A financial professional can help you change strategies when the market isn't going your way, but they won't abandon ship. They will stick to a planful approach. Your retirement isn't based on individual products or investments. It is based on a well-planned strategy that your financial professional is qualified to provide.
- Yellow Money is different from a mutual fund or a 401(k) because, while funds and 401(k)s are investment tools, they are not investment strategies. A 401(k) can be particularly sub-optimal because your employer isn't truly structuring your investments inside the 401(k). They are simply providing you with a few options. The same goes for mutual funds. They are not truly managed by someone who is obligated to have your best interests and your risk tolerance in mind. In fact, the investment strategies of mutual funds change on a regular basis, and you might not know about it until you get an annual report.
- The biggest difference between working with a financial professional to manage your funds, and buying a mutual fund is that, while a mutual fund may buy 20 or more stocks and pegs its earnings on the overall performance of the portfolio,

a financial professional works with you to create an overall financial strategy that meets your needs. It may or may not include mutual funds.

- As an individual investor, do you really have an overarching strategy for your financial portfolio? How did you come up with your selections? Do you know how they are individually managed? Do you know how to make changes to your portfolio that reflect your risk tolerance? Do you know what your risk tolerance is?
- Managed money has specific criteria and a professional will fit that into your overall financial plan so that it works the way you want it to.
- Not all investment firms and financial professionals are created equal. Working with an independent professional will give you options that are customizable to your life.

15
FIXING THE CRACKS IN YOUR NEST EGG

This chapter brings us to the conclusion of my book. Hopefully you will take action to improve your financial, tax, income and wealth distribution planning.

The secret to your success is getting started. If it seems overwhelming and you don't know where to start, answer these questions:

- Does investing seem hard to comprehend?
- Would you rather have someone do it for you?

- Do you <u>not understand</u> what is on your brokerage statement?
- Do you avoid reading about investing or retirement planning because you get stressed?
- How long will your money last?
- Are you overpaying in fees?
- Do you own the right mix of investments that reflect your risk level and objectives?
- Do you have a plan in place to:
    a) Avoid severe losses in the next correction?
    b) Provide more income in the years ahead?
    c) Create retirement income for life in case you lose your job tomorrow (fired, health reasons, etc.)?
    d) Replace lost income if your spouse dies sooner than expected?
    e) Protect your assets from nursing homes taking them all away?

Does your current advisor not service you enough? Does he or she use technology to grow and protect your money? Are you shown reports, illustrations, and information in an easy to understand format?

The keys to wealth are controlled by access: access to resources and the best investments (you'll be limited with captive advisors), access to knowledge (find an advisor who continues to learn), and access to the most current technology (research on investments is helpful but not a pure thing. A program like we use at Lifeguard Financial will watch your money closely and better manage risk, thus minimizing losses).

A comprehensive retirement plan means that you do more than have a lot of investments! It means you have a plan in place to address life's events, a plan to avoid large market losses, a plan to replace the loss of income due to loss of employment and/or loss of a spouse, a plan to guarantee you'll have income even if you live into your 90s, a plan that will provide your children with a monthly check from you for the rest of their lives, after you pass away, a plan to pay for critical care, and a plan to replace costly annuities with riders you may never use.

Most prospects I meet with are like the two pigs in the fairy tale "the three Little Pigs." They go about life and fail to get a fresh perspective on their investments and retirement plan. If they don't think about it then everything is fine. Until it's not fine. One day there will be a loss of income, Social Security may be reduced. They may live into their 90s. Or they may spend hundreds of thousands of dollars on critical care. Their children didn't save for retirement and because there isn't a good distribution plan in place, the children spend the entire inheritance in 90 days and are left with no money for their retirement. They are unknowingly overpaying in fees. When they retire they think they're all set because they have a pension, Social Security and a life insurance policy. Their portfolio contains way too many risky investments and is based on long term investing. Long term! Really? If you're over 65 years old, the long term is behind you! Shorter term investing gives you more flexibility and control. Now is not the time for speculation. Retaining gains with less risk should be your priority.

When it comes to distributing wealth, I hear "I have a trust so I'm all set." All set? In most cases a trust does not shelter your heirs from taxes. Annuities, IRAs and life insurance avoid probate. Why would you name a trust as beneficiary and create higher taxes? Some people need trusts (special needs, multiple businesses or properties, second marriage) and some people can avoid probate with the proper beneficiary designations.

Some people (single, widowed) put their adult child as a joint owner on their accounts. In the event your child gets divorced, goes bankrupt or gets sued, half of your money is subject to the liability. Your child is one-half owner of your money. Instead, get financial and health powers of attorney. This gives your child control when needed and protects your money from lawsuits, divorce, and bankruptcy.

So where are the cracks in your nest egg? Some investors know what needs to be done and do nothing. Some investors don't know and think they are "all set," and some investors do the right thing. They set up a free consultation with a retirement planning expert, receive a detailed analysis, then make the recommended changes to secure their assets. They become the third little pig that built the brick house. They now have peace of mind.

It wasn't raining when Noah built the ark. Yesterday's problems don't have to lead to tomorrow's. What does your plan look like? Is it time for a fresh perspective? What if you could do better? What if you identified the unknown cracks or mistakes in your nest egg and easily could fix them? Having the best person available to guide you to and through retirement should be at the top of your list.

The smart thing to do would be to call me at Lifeguard Financial to discuss what you are currently doing, your goals, and what could be improved. We'll start a profile on you. From there, you'll receive reports that will explain to you in an easy to understand format the Rule of 100:

- What percentage of over exposure you're taking. What dollar amount is at excess risk.
- A Financial CAT Scan that analyzes your investments (quality, performance, duplication, beta, etc.). This identifies what to keep and what to sell.
- How to stop paying for your universal life insurance policy and keep it in force saving thousands of dollars of unnecessary premium.

- Annuity analysis. Do you have a good or bad one? If it's bad, you'll know why and how to exchange it now without penalties or taxes.
- Income Flight Plan. The best way to generate and increase income over time for the rest of your life.
- Replacement Income Analysis. Learn how to create a plan that will be your safety net in case you lose income from an unexpected spousal death or unemployment.
- Stretch IRA Report. Illustrates how to maximize passing your money to your children, avoid unnecessary large taxation, and how to financially set them up for their and your grandchildren's lifetimes.
- Retirement Day. This tells you when you can retire for good. For many, it is much sooner than they realized.
- Social Security Maximization. Find out how to get the most out of what you're entitled to receive.
- Taxable vs Tax Deferred. See how many thousands of dollars you can easily and safely earn on excess money sitting in low interest rate CDs and money market accounts.

There are more reports available that will analyze your situations. The good news is that the facts you will uncover will allow you to make the necessary changes now, before a correction, before you lose a job or spouse, before you give money to children, before you need money for assisted living or a nursing home.

You will not get buried in paperwork. You will receive only the reports that apply to your situation. They're short and easy to read.

In closing, thank you for taking the time to read my book. It shows that you are concerned if you're on track. Your next step will be the most important one in securing your financial future.

Call me at 440-942-1936 to schedule a free consultation at one of our offices close to your home (Mentor, Beachwood, Independence, Westlake, Columbus, in Ohio and Naples, Florida). I'll listen to your concerns and provide you with honest and accurate solutions and recommendations.

I have almost 30 years of experience working with people in their 50s, 60s, 70s, 80s and even 90s. No matter what your age is today, I know what's ahead in the upcoming years for you. Together we can create a more efficient plan that will grow, protect and distribute your assets for generations.

The financial world is a jungle. You need a trusted guide to get you through it. Mastery requires understanding finance, physical mastery and emotional mastery. I am a coach. I prepare you for everything. I am successful not because I am lucky, but because I work hard to do something different and better than everyone else!

"The man at the top of the mountain didn't fall there." - Vince Lombardi.

Financial prosperity is the result of good planning. Again, my direct number is 440-942-1936. Call me today to fix the cracks in your nest egg, and to build wealth while you sleep - each and every day.

THANK YOU FOR READING MY BOOK. I LOOK FORWARD TO HEARING FROM YOU.

Anthony Newman
tn@lifeguardfinancial.com
(440) 942-1936

Learn more about Lifeguard Financial and our services at www.lifeguardfinancial.com. Visit our video library and sign up for our next informative and educational retirement planning seminar. Better yet, call Lifeguard Financial today at (440) 942-1936 for a free consultation and second opinion to see if you are on track.

GLOSSARY

ANNUAL RESET *(ANNUAL RATCHET, CLIQUET)* – Crediting methods measuring index movement over a one year period. Positive interest is calculated and credited at the end of each contract year and cannot be lost if the index subsequently declines. Say that the index increased from 100 to 110 in one year and the indexed annuity had an 80 percent participation rate. The insurance company would take the 10 percent gross index gain for the year (110-100/100), apply the participation rate (10 percent index gain x 80 percent rate) and credit 8 percent interest to the annuity. But, what if in the following year the index declined back to 100? The individual would keep the 8 percent interest earned and simply receive zero interest for the down year. An annual reset structure preserves credited gains and treats negative index periods as years with zero growth.

ANNUITANT – The person, usually the annuity owner, whose life expectancy is used to calculate the income payment amount on the annuity.

ANNUITY – An annuity is a contract issued by an insurance company that often serves as a type of savings plan used by individuals looking for long term growth and protection of assets that will likely be needed within retirement.

AVERAGING – Index values may either be measured from a start point to an end point (point-to-point) or values between the start point and end point may be averaged to determine an ending value. Index values may be averaged over the days, weeks, months or quarters of the period.

BENEFICIARY – A beneficiary is the person designated to receive payments due upon the death of the annuity owner or the annuitant themselves.

BONUS RATE – A bonus rate is the "extra" or "additional" interest paid during the first year (the initial guarantee period), typically used as an added incentive to get consumers to select their annuity policy over another.

CALL OPTION *(ALSO SEE PUT OPTION)* – Gives the holder the right to buy an underlying security or index at a specified price on or before a given date.

CAP – The maximum interest rate that will be credited to the annuity for the year or period. The cap usually refers to the maximum interest credited after applying the participation rate or yield spread. If the index methodology showed a 20 percent increase, the participation rate was 60 percent and the maximum interest cap was 10 percent, the contract would credit 10 percent interest. A few annuities use a maximum gain cap instead of a maximum interest cap with the participation rate or yield spread applied to the lesser of the gain or the cap. If the index methodology showed a 20 percent increase, the participation rate was 60 percent and the maximum gain cap was 10 percent, the contract would credit 6 percent interest.

COMPOUND INTEREST – Interest is earned on both the original principal and on previously earned interest. It is more favorable than simple interest. Suppose that your original principal was $1 and your interest rate was 10 percent for five years. With simple interest, your value is ($1 + $0.10 interest each year) = $1.50. With compound interest, your value is ($1 x 1.10 x 1.10 x 1.10 x 1.10 x 1.10) = $1.61. The advantage of compound interest over simple interest becomes greater as each subsequent period passes.

CREDITING METHOD *(ALSO SEE METHODOLOGY)* – The formula(s) used to determine the excess interest that is credited above the minimum interest guarantee.

DEATH BENEFITS – The payment the annuity owner's estate or beneficiaries will receive if he or she dies before the annuity matures. On most annuities, this is equal to the current account value. Some annuities offer an enhanced value at death via an optional rider that has a monthly or annual fee associated with it.

EXCESS INTEREST – Interest credited to the annuity contract above the minimum guaranteed interest rate. In an indexed annuity the excess interest is determined by applying a stated crediting method to a specific index or indices.

FIXED ANNUITY – A contract issued by an insurance company guaranteeing a minimum interest rate with the crediting of excess interest determined by the performance of the insurer's general account. Index annuities are fixed annuities.

FIXED DEFERRED ANNUITY – With fixed annuities, an insurance company offers a guaranteed interest rate plus safety of your principal and earnings ((subject to the claims-paying ability of the insurance company). Your interest rate will be reset periodically, based on economic and other factors, but is guaranteed to never fall below a certain rate.

FREE WITHDRAWALS – Withdrawals that are free of surrender charges.

INDEX – The underlying external benchmark upon which the crediting of excess interest is based, also a measure of the prices of a group of securities.

IRA *(INDIVIDUAL RETIREMENT ACCOUNT)* – An IRA is a tax-advantaged personal savings plan that lets an individual set aside money for retirement. All or part of the participant's contributions may be tax deductible, depending on the type of IRA chosen and the participant's personal financial circumstances. Distributions from many employer-sponsored retirement plans may be eligible to be rolled into an IRA to continue tax-deferred growth until the funds are needed. An annuity can be used as an IRA; that is, IRA funds can be used to purchase an annuity.

IRA ROLLOVER – IRA rollover is the phrase used when an individual who has a balance in an employer-sponsored retirement plan transfers that balance into an IRA. Such an exchange, when properly handled, is a tax-advantaged transaction.

LIQUIDITY – The ease with which an asset is convertible to cash. An asset with high liquidity provides flexibility, in that the owner can easily convert it to cash at any time, but it also tends to decrease profitability.

MARKET RISK – The risk of the market value of an asset fluctuating up or down over time. In a fixed or fixed indexed annuity, the original principal and credited interest are not subject to market risk. Even if the index declines, the annuity owner would receive no less than their original principal back if they decided to cash in the policy at the end of the surrender period. Unlike a security, indexed annuities guarantee the original premium and the premium is backed by, and is as safe as, the insurance company that issued it (subject to the claims-paying ability of the insurance company).

METHODOLOGY *(ALSO SEE CREDITING METHOD)* – The way that interest crediting is calculated. On fixed indexed annuities, there are a variety of different methods used to determine how index movement becomes interest credited.

MINIMUM GUARANTEED RETURN *(MINIMUM INTEREST RATE)* – Fixed indexed annuities typically provide a minimum guaranteed return over the life of the contract. At the time that the owner chooses to terminate the contract, the cash surrender value is compared to a second value calculated using the minimum guaranteed return and the higher of the two values is paid to the annuity owner.

OPTION – A contract which conveys to its holder the right, but not the obligation, to buy or sell something at a specified price on or before a given date. After this given date the option ceases to exist. Insurers typically buy options to provide for the excess interest potential. Options may be American style whereby they may be exercised at any time prior to the given date, or they may have to be exercised only during a specified window. Options that may only be exercised during a specified period are European-style options.

OPTION RISK – Most insurers create the potential for excess interest in an indexed annuity by buying options. Say that you could buy a share of stock for $50. If you bought the stock and it rose to $60 you could sell it and net a $10 profit. But, if the stock price fell to $40 you'd have a $10 loss. Instead of buying the actual stock, we could buy an option that gave us the right to buy the stock for $50 at any time over the next year. The cost of the option is $2. If the stock price rose to $60 we would exercise our option, buy the stock at $50 and make $10 (less the $2 cost of the option). If the price of the stock fell to $40, $30 or $10, we wouldn't use the option and it would expire. The loss is limited to $2 – the cost of the option.

PARTICIPATION RATE – The percentage of positive index movement credited to the annuity. If the index methodology determined that the index increased 10 percent and the indexed annuity participated in 60 percent of the increase, it would be said that the contract has a 60 percent participation rate. Participation rates may also be expressed as asset fees or yield spreads.

POINT-TO-POINT – A crediting method measuring index movement from an absolute initial point to the absolute end point for a period. An index had a period starting value of 100 and a period ending value of 120. A point-to-point method would record a positive index movement of 20 [120-100] or a 20 percent positive movement [(120-100)/100]. Point-to-point usually refers to annual periods; however the phrase is also used instead of term end point to refer to multiple year periods.

PREMIUM BONUS – A premium bonus is additional money that is credited to the accumulation account of an annuity policy under certain conditions.

PUT OPTION *(ALSO SEE CALL OPTION)* – Gives the holder the right to sell an underlying security or index at a specified price on or before a given date.

QUALIFIED ANNUITIES *(QUALIFIED MONEY)* – Qualified annuities are annuities purchased for funding an IRA, 403(b) tax-deferred annuity or other type of retirement arrangements. An IRA or qualified retirement plan provides the tax deferral. An annuity contract should be used to fund an IRA or qualified retirement plan to benefit from an annuity's features other than tax deferral, including the safety features, lifetime income payout option and death benefit protection.

REQUIRED MINIMUM DISTRIBUTION *(RMD)* – The amount of money that Traditional, SEP and SIMPLE IRA owners and qualified plan participants must begin distributing from their retirement accounts by April 1 following the year they reach age 70.5. RMD amounts must then be distributed each subsequent year.

RETURN FLOOR – Another way of saying minimum guaranteed return.

ROTH IRA – Like other IRA accounts, the Roth IRA is simply a holding account that manages your stocks, bonds, annuities, mutual funds and CD's. However, future withdrawals (including earnings and interest) are typically tax-advantaged once the account has been open for five years and the account holder is age 59.5.

RULE OF 72 – Tells you approximately how many years it takes a sum to double at a given rate. It's handy to be able to figure out, without using a calculator, that when you're earning a 6 percent return, for example, by dividing 6 percent into 72, you'll find that it takes 12 years for money to double. Conversely, if you know it took a sum twelve years to double you could divide 12 into 72 to determine the annual return (6 percent).

SIMPLE INTEREST *(ALSO SEE COMPOUND INTEREST)* – Interest is only earned on the principal balance.

SPLIT ANNUITY – A split annuity is the term given to an effective strategy that utilizes two or more different annuity products – one designed to generate monthly income and the other to restore the original starting principal over a set period of time.

STANDARD & POOR'S 500 *(S&P 500)* – The most widely used external index by fixed indexed annuities. Its objective is to be a benchmark to measure and report overall U.S. stock market performance. It includes a representative sample of 500 common stocks from companies trading on the New York Stock Exchange, American Stock Exchange, and NASDAQ National Market System. The index represents the price or market value of the underlying stocks and does not include the value of reinvested dividends of the underlying stocks.

STOCK MARKET INDEX – A report created from a type of statistical measurement that shows up or down changes in a specific financial market, usually expressed as points and as a percentage, in a number of related markets, or in an economy as a whole (i.e. S&P 500 or New York Stock Exchange).

SURRENDER CHARGE – A charge imposed for withdrawing funds or terminating an annuity contract prematurely. There is no industry standard for surrender charges, that is, each annuity product has its own unique surrender charge schedule. The charge is usually expressed as a percentage of the amount withdrawn prematurely from the contract. The percentage tends to decline over time, ultimately becoming zero.

TRADITIONAL IRA – See <u>IRA (Individual Retirement Account)</u>

TERM END POINT – Crediting methods measuring index movements over a greater timeframe than a year or two. The opposite of an annual reset method. Also referred to as a term point-to-point method. Say that the index value was at 100 on the first day of the period. If the calculated index value was at 150 at the end of the period the positive index movement would be 50 percent (150-100/100). The company would credit a percentage of this movement as excess interest. Index movement is calculated and interest credited at the end of the term and interim movements during the period are ignored.

TERM HIGH POINT *(HIGH WATER MARK)* – A type of term end point structure that uses the highest anniversary index level as the end point. Say that the index value was at 100 on the first day of the period, reached a value of 160 at the end of a contract year during the period, and ended the period at 150. A term high point method would use the 160 value – the highest contract anniversary point reached during the period, as the end point and the gross index gain would be 60 percent (160-100/100). The company would then apply a participation rate to the gain.

TERM YIELD SPREAD – A type of term end point structure which calculates the total index gain for a period, computes the annual compound rate of return deducts a yield spread from the annual rate of return and then recalculates the total index gain for the period based on the net annual rate. Say that an index increased from 100 to 200 by the end of a nine year period. This is the equivalent of an 8 percent compound annual interest rate. If the annuity had a 2 percent term yield spread this would be deducted from the annual interest rate (8 percent-2 percent) and the net rate would be credited to the contract (6 percent) for each of the nine years. Total index gain may also be computed by using the highest anniversary index level as the end point.

VARIABLE ANNUITY – A contract issued by an insurance company offering separate accounts invested in a wide variety of stocks and/or bonds. The investment risk is borne by the annuity owner. Variable annuities are considered securities and require appropriate securities registration.

1035 EXCHANGE – The 1035 exchange refers to the section of tax code that allows annuity owners the flexibility to exchange one annuity for another without incurring any immediate tax liabilities. This action is most often utilized when an annuity holder decides they want to upgrade an annuity to a more favorable one, but they do not want to activate unnecessary tax liabilities that would typically be encountered when surrendering an existing annuity contract.

401(K) ROLLOVER – See <u>IRA Rollover</u>

There's a Crack in Your Nest Egg

Inheritance Taxes to Children

Too Much Risk/Large Losses

Low Interest Rates

Loss of Spouse & Income

Outliving Your Money

High Fees

Annual Taxes

Nursing Homes

Taxes on IRA RMD's

Inflation

Outdated or No Will/Trust

Insurance Premiums

If any of these relate to you, call